The Deranged Stalker's

Journal of *Pop Culture* *Shock Therapy*

The Deranged Stalker's

Journal of *Pop Culture* Shock Therapy

by Doug Bratton

Andrews McMeel
Publishing, LLC
Kansas City • Sydney • London

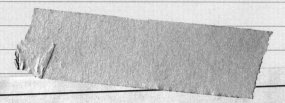

10 11 12 13 14 RR2 10 9 8 7 6 5 4 3 2 1

ISBN: 978-0-7407-9904-4

Library of Congress Control Number: 2010924504

www.andrewsmcmeel.com

Attention: Schools and Businesses
Andrews McMeel books are available at quantity discounts with
bulk purchase for educational, business, or sales promotional use.
For information, please write to: Special Sales Department,
Andrews McMeel Publishing, LLC, 1130 Walnut Street,
Kansas City, Missouri 64106.

Introduction

All stories have a beginning, and the story of how this book came to be starts as so
many others have—with someone (in this case, me and my family) receiving a death
threat from a homicidal lunatic and his imaginary friend "Bob."

Actually, in some ways, that's how the story ends. It would probably make sense
for me to give you a bit of background on who I am and what *Pop Culture Shock
Therapy* is, because there is a high likelihood that you've never heard of either prior to
holding this book (unless you are a relative of mine, went to school with me, happened
across *Pop Culture Shock Therapy* while surfing the Web when your boss wasn't around,
or have attended one of about 50 colleges in the United States over the past several
years that has had the excellent taste to run this comic in its campus newspaper).

So I am Doug Bratton, 30-something-year-old cartoonist, and *Pop Culture Shock
Therapy* is a daily newspaper (yes, at the time of this writing, they do still exist) comic
panel that parodies entertainment-media, such as television, movies, superheroes,
cartoons, music, and celebrities. It is satirical in nature, viewing the world through the
lens of current and 20th-century popular culture, which for better or worse, influences
most of us more than we'd care to admit. I started the comic online in 2002, and
shortly thereafter began syndicating it to college newspapers. (It first appeared in
print in 2003 in Rutgers University's *Daily Targum*—shoutout!)

Over the years, *Pop Culture Shock Therapy* has built a fan base of readers online,
through these newspapers, and at comic conventions where I exhibit, sell, and speak.
It is not uncommon for readers to e-mail me if they particularly like—or are offended

by—a comic. I am not overwhelmed by e-mails, although I do receive them consistently, and so I respond to all of them. This is how Dan (the stalker) and "Bob" first came into my life.

I don't want to give away too many of the details—you can read them for yourself in this book—but as it turns out, Dan had been keeping a journal of my comics for several years before reaching out to me. To say Dan's e-mails were odd might be understating things a bit. By his second or third e-mail, I had to stop writing back. Shortly after that, I had to go to the police, and not long after that, Dan was taken into custody. When the police raided Dan's apartment in the basement of his mother's home, they found, well, lots of creepy things that you might expect to find in the apartment of a criminally insane person. Among the weirdness was a box of over 1,000 *Pop Culture Shock Therapy* comics that Dan had apparently ripped out of a local college newspaper by hand (I'll leave out the name of that college for obvious reasons), and a journal that he began to keep at some point, revolved around the comics.

The police gave me a copy of the journal, and somehow word of the "deranged cartoonist stalker" found its way into the local and national media (although you may have missed it—something happened with Tiger Woods and an SUV crash around the same time that overshadowed the story for some reason). From there, things kind of snowballed.

I received a call from Caty Neis (now my editor) at Andrews McMeel Universal within a week of the media firestorm. As it turns out, editors are always on the lookout for book ideas that might sell a few thousand copies, and tabloid media stories about deranged stalkers apparently help sell books. Bottom line: Andrews McMeel was EXTREMELY interested in publishing Dan's journal, and because the vast majority of the work within it was mine, I legally owned the copyright to it.

While I was thrilled that Andrews McMeel was interested in publishing a collection of *Pop Culture Shock Therapy* comics, I have to admit, I did have a few concerns. First, would people want to read this book because of my comics, or because of the added bizarre rambling of some nut-job? Second, this Dan guy is now going to prison, and something is clearly not right within his mind. Would allowing this journal to go to print somehow be exploiting mental illness? I made these concerns known to Caty, who immediately gave me an impassioned speech about this legally being my work, how the unique nature of the "stalker" story would create "buzz" for the book, how this "buzz" could lead to a place on the "*New York Times* Bestseller List," how "selling out" is really just another way of saying "selling lots of copies," which means "making a lot of money," and on and on and on.

Truthfully, around the time I heard the phrase "making a lot of money" all of those concerns about artistic integrity and exploitation just seemed to fade magically away. A few quick contract negotiations, some conversations about book publicity and speaking engagements, and voila!—you are now reading a copy of *The Deranged Stalker's Journal of Pop Culture Shock Therapy*. One can only expect that the chances of law enforcement coming across additional journals is somehow directly related to the number of copies that this baby sells, so be sure you make this book the only thing you give out as a Christmas/Hanukkah/birthday/Valentine/Easter/wedding present this year.

It is my great hope that you enjoy not only Dan's story as it unfolds throughout the pages of the book, but also the comics that inspired him to want to hunt me down and kill me. It is also my hope that it does not inspire you to do the same. My lawn can only take so many people hiding in the bushes with binoculars.

—Doug Bratton

June 2010

AN ADDED NOTE TO THE READER: If, by some chance, you happen across this book in the tiny "Humor" section of your local bookstore, clearly, there was some clerical error, or a dim-witted fool who did not fully understand the significance or importance of this work misplaced the book. You can do everyone a big favor by simply purchasing this copy and placing all other copies back in the front of the store under the sign "*New York Times* #1 Nonfiction Best Seller" in front of whatever Malcolm Gladwell book was haphazardly thrown up there. On behalf of this bookstore, I kindly thank you in advance for your assistance.

For Pam and Caden, with love.

Thank you for your patience, love, support, and understanding over the years while this dream took root.

Also, I'm sorry about the death threats and the crazy guy in the bushes.

"I had that strange dream again, Bert. You know . . .
the one where you get dressed up like a gorilla in
the middle of the night and beat me with a baseball bat."

Went to Court-Appointed Psychologist (moron) with Bob (friend).
Bob saw this comic in newspaper. He ripped it out for me. I liked it
(reminded me of Mother).

I like Bob and Bob is my only friend and I do not like other people
who are not Bob.

Can't talk to Court-Appointed Psychologist about Bob.
Court-Appointed Psychologist says he can't see Bob and Bob is not
real and will ask why I think I can see Bob and will accuse me of
not taking medication (parole violation).

When Cartoon Fights Turn Ugly

Back at Court-Appointed Psychologist office (must visit 3 times per week). Bob ripped another comic out for me. Bob is a good friend and is not like Mother. Bob is nice to me and doesn't scream at me and lock me in the closet and tell me not to eat his peanut butter.

Bob and I like this comic so I will rip out comics and make a book for myself and Bob (free). I make lots of things myself (pants, soap, lawn mowers, toothpaste, etc.). People should not buy toilet paper when old newspapers are free at recycling center.

Eeyore's Lesser-Seen Manic State

Things I can buy with money I don't spend on a book:
1. binoculars
2. giant tub of beef jerky (Slim Jims)
3. duct tape & binding twine
4. bonesaw
5. T-shirt of howling wolves

Sir Mix-a-Lot in High School English Class

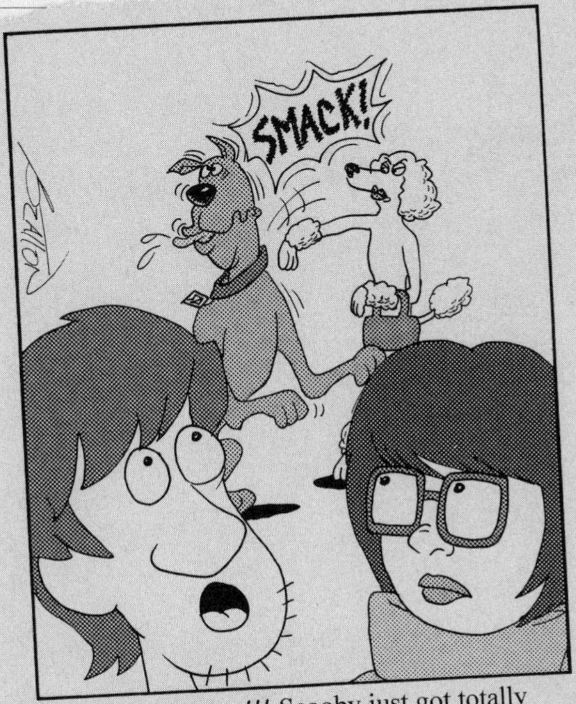
SMACK!

"*Daaaaammmn!!!* Scooby just got totally bitch-slapped!"

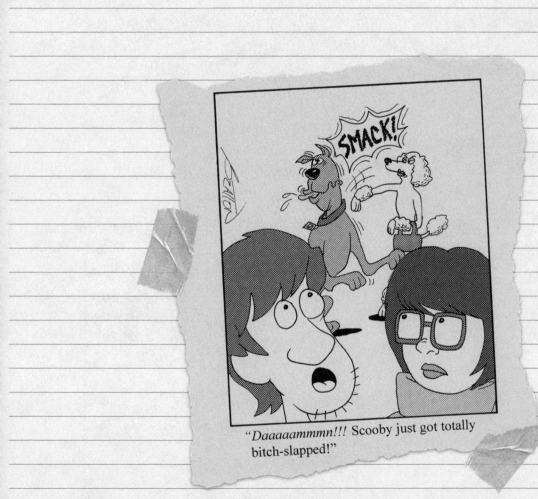

Fast Food, Faster Women

"Hold on a minute . . . We were supposed to surgically remove the patient's *tentacles?!* Well, *this* guy's not gonna be too happy when he wakes up."

Can relate to this comic, but not allowed to own guns and other
"weapon-like objects" (court order).

Earliest memories of Mother:
1. Wearing clown costume (drunk)
2. Getting me a pack of Kools for birthday present
3. Waking me up in the middle of the night to help move furniture
   in front of door so that vampires couldn't get in the house

"Well, *that* was disappointing."

William Tell's court-appointed social worker always seemed to ruin his good times.

Court-Appointed Social Workers are not fun and tell you what you can't do and ask too many questions and make direct eye contact.

The Ahoy's were deathly mistaken—there *was* a
monster in little Chip's closet: a Cookie Monster!

Things Court-Appointed Social Workers said I can't do:

1. Drive a car
2. Go within 500 ft. of school
3. Go to "G" or "PG" movies (can go to PG-13 with court permission)
4. Go to malls
5. Purchase matches, cutlery, or piano wire (interpreted as "weapon-like")
6. Be a sperm donor
7. Own cats anymore
8. Take karate

Tarzan in Celebrity Rehab

After "Crazy" was kicked out, the remaining seven Dwarfs became the group commonly known today.

I do not understand why roommates get upset and want you to "move out before tonight" when you talk to them about stuff. Bob is the only roommate that does not get mad when I tell him about stuff and says I should not tell other people stuff because they will say mean things like "you are crazy" or "maybe you need to get some help" or "you are making me uncomfortable."

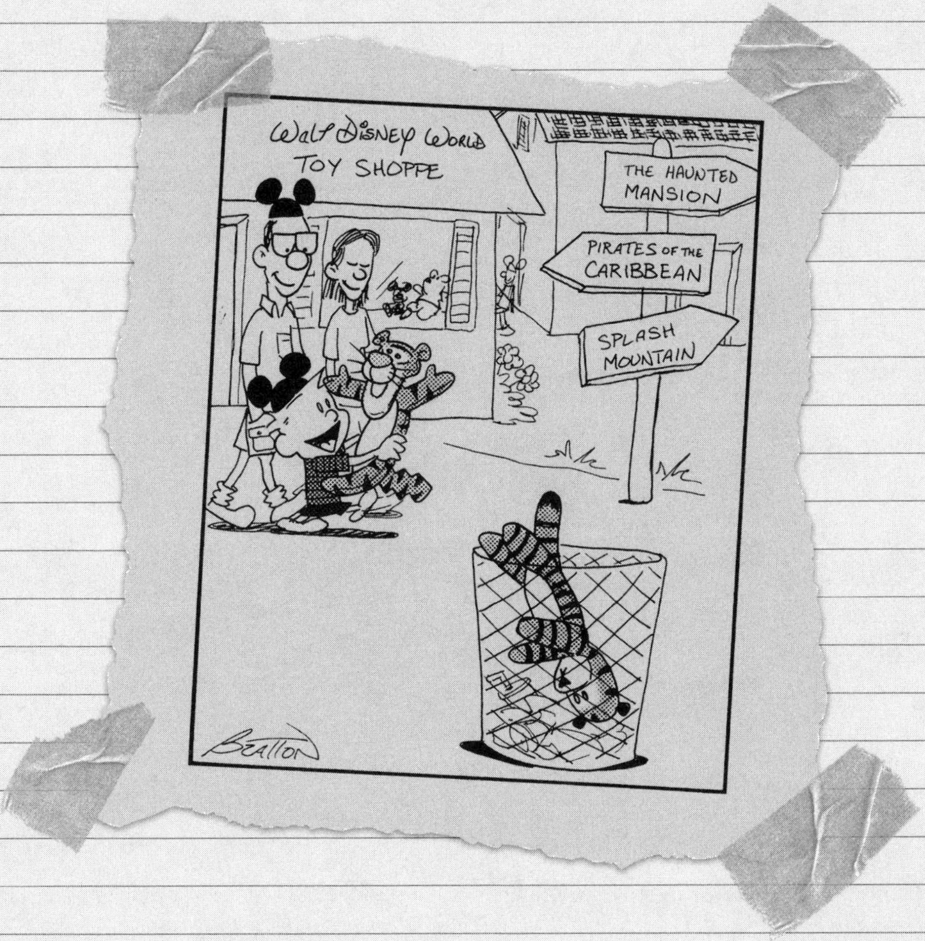
WALT DISNEY WORLD
TOY SHOPPE
THE HAUNTED MANSION
PIRATES OF THE CARIBBEAN
SPLASH MOUNTAIN
BEATTON

"Death," "Apathy," and "Satan Worshipper"
just didn't seem to fit in with the other Care Bears.

Dear *Pop Culture Shock Therapy* Cartoonist,

I enjoy reading your comics and find them to be funny. I am tearing them out of the newspaper and save them and my friend Bob and I look at them and Bob thinks they are funny too.

In a recent comic, you have several Care Bears that include "Death," Apathy," and "Satan Worshipper." When I was little I made my own Care Bears and had made these same (Care Bears) and more, including Fire Starter Bear, Suffocation Bear (pillow on stomach), Wet the Bed Bear, etc. I was wondering if by chance you know my Mother and she told you about these bears and that gave you the idea for this comic? If so, did she tell you other things about me? Sometimes she tells lies.

I am a big fan of your *Pop Culture Shock Therapy* comics and think it is funny how you kill characters that I know. I will send you some comic ideas that I draw in the mail and you can use them but I would like my name added to the comics. Have you been making comics for a long time? What other things do you like to do besides making comics? Where do you live? Do you live alone? Do you have kids? Where do they go to school? What things do they like (i.e., candy, toys)?

Bob and I really like your comics and hope to come see you someday.

Sincerely,
Dan

Hi Dan,

So glad to hear you and Bob enjoy the comics. And sadly, no, I don't know your mom—just a coincidence that we had the same Care Bear ideas. I guess great minds think alike! Thanks for the offer to send ideas for the comic, but unfortunately I can't use them from other people (with the exception of my brother and one or two close friends)—this way I don't get sued if a comic goes on to make millions! LOL

Thanks for taking the time to write, and thanks again for your kind words about the comics. (And please feel free to call me Doug!)

Best regards,
Doug

Not sure if I can believe that Pop Culture Shock Therapy Cartoonist doesn't know Mother. Nice of him to say I should call him "Doug" but I will not as I only call Bob his first name, no one else (too humanizing).

Keebler Homophobia

Everyone soon learned that Theodor Seuss Geisel was a dirty, stinking liar.

EDGE
Where the Sidewalk Ends
POEMS · SONGS · BODY DUMPING

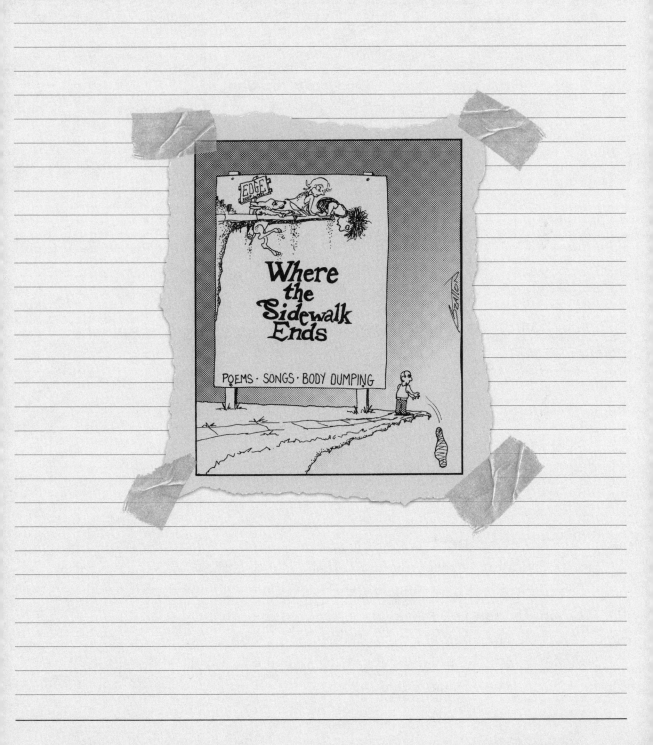

Happy Mother's Day from Mr. Spock

Why I love Mother:
1. She is not home a lot
2. Lets me eat bacon

Why I hate Mother:
1. Always watches me and tells people lies about me to make them hate me (i.e., chipmunk and Christmas lights story)
2. Tries to poison me
3. Ignores Bob
4. Throws lit firecrackers on my bed to wake me up (startles me and sometimes burns)

Oscar, before the Gambling Addiction

"There's no place like home . . . there's no place lik—wait a minute. What the hell am I saying?! I'm from *Kansas*!!!"

Stayed at a motel in Kansas once. There was a loud woman with a lot of eye makeup outside the ice machine who kept trying to get me to talk to her and give her money to buy beer and then she asked me if I needed some company and tried to make direct eye contact with me so I left the motel and didn't pay.

In Candyland, kids trick-or-treat for protein.

The Human Torch's Parents

Do not understand why some people (Court-Appointed
Psychologist) get so upset if you play with fire. Fire is very bright
and yellow and glowy and I wrote a poem about how much
I loved fire in 3rd grade and then I got sent away for testing.

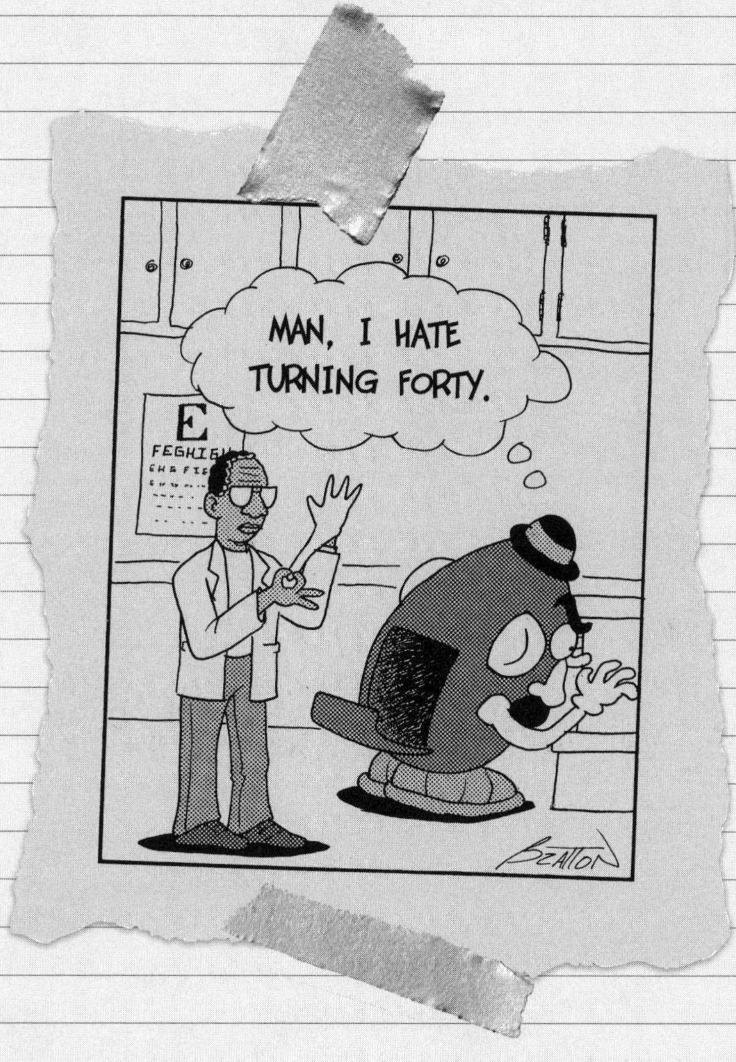
MAN, I HATE TURNING FORTY.
BEATTON

"Check it out, Robin: *plumber's crack*. That, my friend, is why we wear capes."

C.S.I. Tatooine

Wish Stormtroopers showed up at my house and found Mother
instead of robots with Death Star plans. That would teach Mother
not to wear her clown costume and try to poison me.
Also wish I had a robot.

Count Dracula forgot about
Daylight Savings Time—did you?

It took Superman nine tries before he figured
out what Hester Prynne's scarlet letter stood for.

The never-before-seen postlude to the
Tootsie Roll Pop Commercial

Things that make me feel like hitting someone with an ax:

1. When Court-Appointed Psychiatrists try and ask me questions about Bob and it gets me in trouble for not taking medication

2. When people at grocery store don't put their shopping carts back and just leave them in the parking lot

3. When Mothers are drunk and throw firecrackers

4. When Bob leaves the toilet seat up

Ziggy's Criminally Insane Twin Brother, Zoggy

Bob says this comic reminds him of me when we fight over toilet seat issues but I do not look anything like Ziggy (have hair, smallish nose).

Little Popeye was not careful.

Aquaman's Funeral

The Comedy Stylings of
Charlie "Chuckles" Manson

Told Bob I like this guy's style. Bob says I'm "crazy" and I don't like it when people call me the "C word" especially not my neighbor who said she saw me looking in her window from the bushes outside her house when really I was just trying to find a good hiding spot because sometimes people are out to get me. DON'T EVER CALL ME CRAZY BOB DON'T EVER EVER EVER EVER EVER EVER CALL ME CRAZY OR I WILL GET YOU.

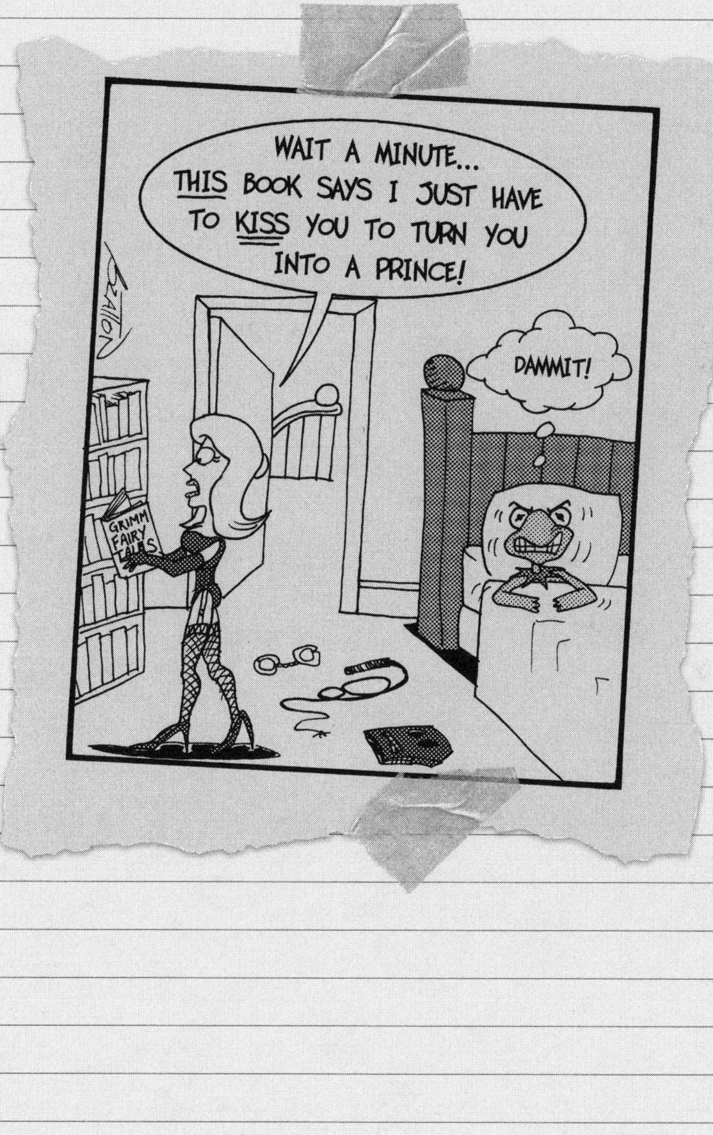
WAIT A MINUTE...
THIS BOOK SAYS I JUST HAVE TO KISS YOU TO TURN YOU INTO A PRINCE!
DAMMIT!
GRIMM FAIRY TALES
BEATON

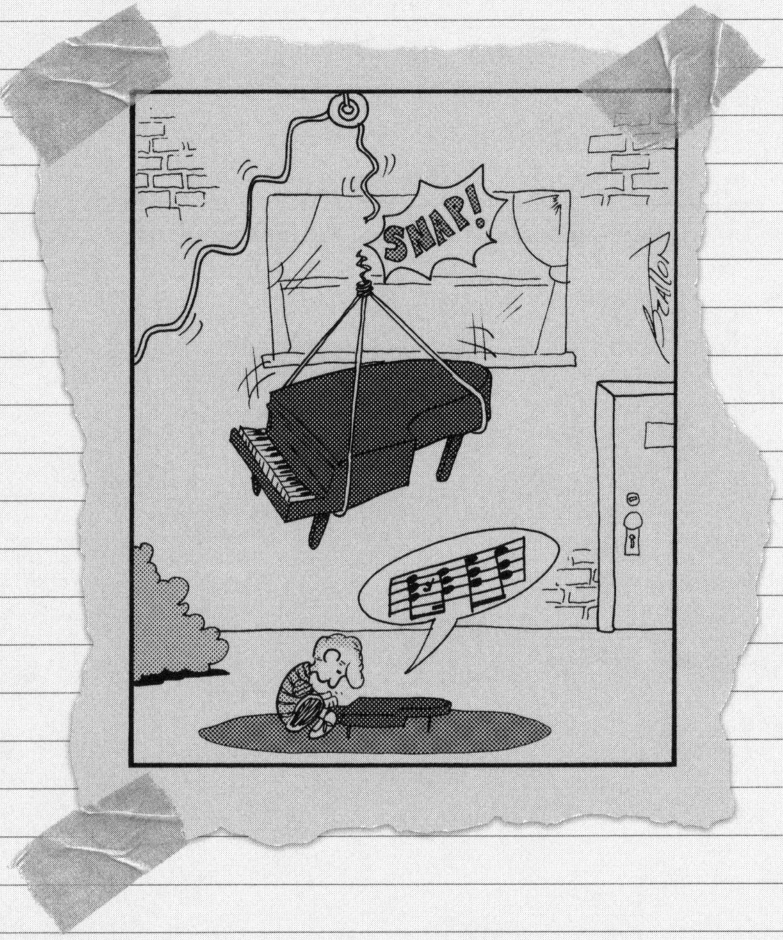
SNAP!

If Marilyn Manson Won the Superbowl

Templeton Reveals Charlotte's Web of Lies

Unfortunately, because of thermonuclear annihilation, Annie is mistaken.

First Dates with O. J. Simpson

Had a date like this once. Did not go well. Never talk about past criminal charges with women, especially on first date (that's a third date conversation, IF EVER).

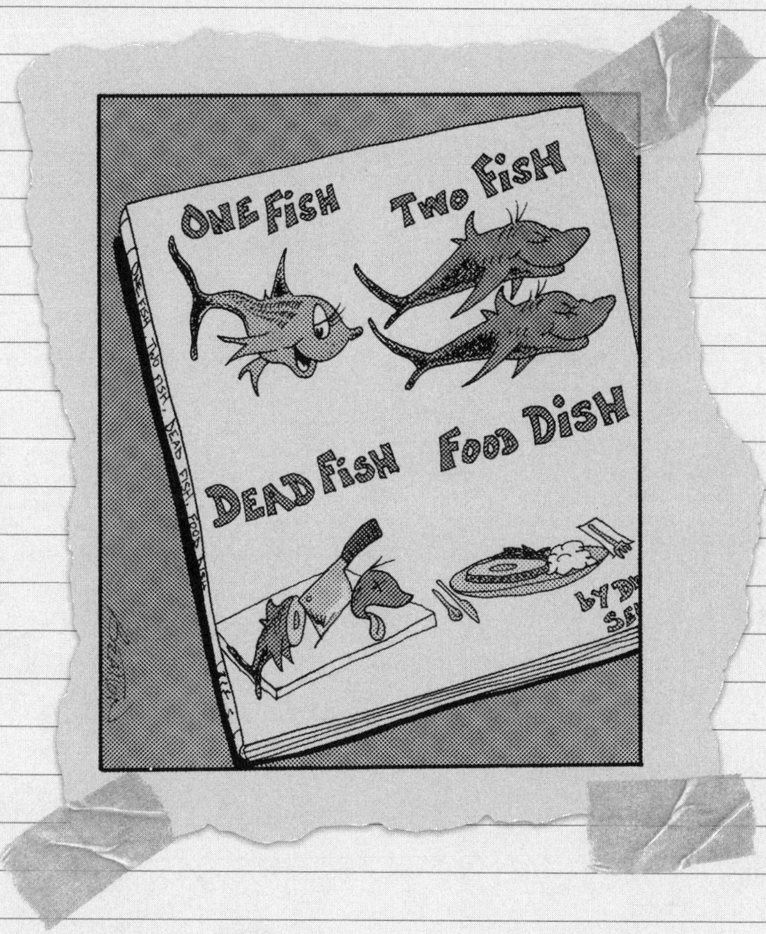
ONE FISH
TWO FISH
DEAD FISH
FOOD DISH

Walt Disney's *Fargo*

One second later, the entire universe imploded.

Pooh eventually grew tired with being called
"a bear of very little brain."

Things that make me want to hit someone with a bat:
1. When someone in store asks if they can help me find something
2. When someone tries to get me in trouble for looking in her window
3. When loud women try to make direct eye contact
4. When someone tells me I can call him by his first name

Even though the school would never say, the students all knew who had started the lice epidemic.

After reading this comic, told Bob that I think Mother might know Pop Culture Shock Therapy Cartoonist and may be telling him stories about me to use in comics. First the Care Bears and now this.

Why Cereal Cartoon Mascots Hate French People

J.K. Rowling's Private Washroom

The First Day That the Comic Strip *Cathy*
Is Taken Over by Men

She really does talk a lot.

The Previously Untold Origin of
Casper the Friendly Ghost

The Last Thing Little Max Saw, after Getting Too Comfortable with the Wild Things

Christopher Robin struggled with alcohol and mental health problems in his adult years.

Cannot imagine what I would do if I found out my best friend in the world wasn't real. Would probably go crazy.

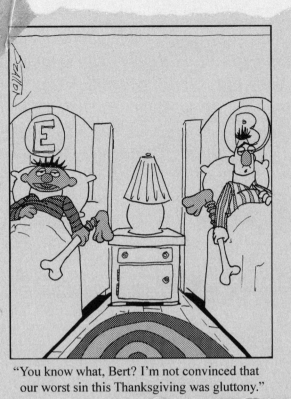

"You know what, Bert? I'm not convinced that
our worst sin this Thanksgiving was gluttony."

"Hey, kids, see those ghosts?
They touch you, you die."

Asked Bob if he thought it was wrong to attack your parent with an ax if the parent was very mean and threw firecrackers at you and tried to poison you and Bob asked if I was referring to Mother and I said no I was just wondering.

Spider-man's Narcolepsy

Mr. Spock on Anti-Depressants

Anti-depressants are not helpful. They just make you hungry and dizzy and hear voices inside your brain and want to shave the cat.

Peter Pan never again worried about having to catch his shadow.

Superheroes usually tune out their mandatory
Non-Violent Conflict Resolution Class.

Court-Appointed Social Workers mandate these classes.
I wish there were superheroes in my classes but there are just
people who smell bad and get really angry if you sit in their
favorite chair.

Finding Nemo Dead

Painful reminder of the loss of the closest friend I ever had (until Bob). Had a pet goldfish and his name was Chubby and when he died I couldn't bring myself to flush him down the toilet, so now he is in a jar of formaldehyde under my bed.

Paul Bunyan never really got over the accidental crushing death of the Old Lady Who Lived in a Shoe.

When School Nurses Mail It In

Pinocchio realizes that life would be much more
fun without a conscience.

Doc, having recently received his Ph.D. in psychology, rediagnoses his housemates.

"Maybe *NOW* he'll finally understand that Trix are for kids."

Bob says we should only live in states that don't have the death penalty in case there is ever a big misunderstanding and we are wrongly accused of doing something very very very bad.

Ultimately, Ken would go home to Barbie frustrated, humiliated, and without thirty dollars.

Can't do this (Court-Appointed Social Worker said so). If Bob and I both went three times a day we could make some goooooooood money.

Adam wasn't going to let Snow White make the same mistake that he had made.

Charlie and the Chocolate Factory in His Shorts

I do not think it is funny to make jokes about times when people have accidents because sometimes people just have bad dreams when they are sleeping about Mothers throwing firecrackers at them or trying to poison them or running in the room in a clown costume screaming about vampires and they wake up and it just happened.

Suddenly, Mr. Potato Head began to put all of the pieces together: the sour cream … the butter … the "Jacuzzi."

When He-Man and Skeletor Stand before God

Do not understand why anyone would ever pay for a psychiatrist.
Court-Appointed Psychiatrists are free.

Marvel Bad Guy Men's Room

Bambi's Revenge

"Seriously, I #@&%ing *hate* kids."

Bob likes this comic because he does not like kids. Bob says kids are nothing but trouble because they make fun of you and call you names and when you catch them and put shackles on them and force them to do yard work for you their parents get upset and call the police and you can get charged with wrongful imprisonment and endangering a minor.

Whenever someone has an ax and no heart,
something terrible is bound to happen.

Have already discussed feelings on ax attacks.

Other things that make me want to hit someone with an ax:
1. When people cut in front of me in line.
2. When Bob eats all the bacon.
3. Chipmunks.

Everyone froze—no one had ever ordered a certain appetizer when a certain friend was present.

Bil Keane's loveless marriage began to creep into his work.

Fertility Doctor Smurf

When the Joker Takes His Anti-Psychotic Meds

Why I won't take anti-psychotic medication:
1. Makes me too happy
2. Has "salty" taste
3. Bob goes away when I use it
4. Side effect risks
5. Can't operate heavy machinery or my arms

No Justice League member ever brought
seafood to the annual superhero picnic again.

How Andy Capp Lost His
Commercial Airline Pilot Job

Why I will no longer eat anything Mother cooks (will sometimes eat bacon). Bob says my just sitting there and refusing to eat her food makes him feel very uncomfortable each night at dinnertime. Bob says a lot of things I do make him uncomfortable.

Kirk was always extra careful to make sure he flushed in order to avoid any bad "Captain's Log" jokes.

"The best part of being a Disney character is
that I'm *always* guaranteed a happy ending."

I do not go to massage parlors because I DO NOT WANT ANYONE
UNDER ANY CIRCUMSTANCES EVER TO TOUCH ME.

"Bring Your Cat to Work Day" ended up costing
the Disney Company millions.

Superheroes after the Senate Crackdown
on Steroid Use

Bob says that someday I'll understand this comic and then starts crying (aaawwwkkkward).

Cinderella's husband learns why you never
marry a hottie after just one date.

Bad place to dump a body. Too much open space.

When Superheroes Lose Their Motivation

Wookie Pattern Baldness

Bob says Bert reminds him of me in these comics.
I think it is because we are roommates.

On a bad tip from his agent, Grimace shows up
for *The Color Purple* auditions.

The Bad News Bears

Bob says you can get in big trouble for putting a ladder up to someone's window, even if you just climb up and look and never go inside.

Dagwood's "Brunett-ie" Fantasy

The Red Cross eventually figured out that Superman was just showing up for the free cookies.

Can relate to wanting to rip Court-Appointed Psychiatrist's arms off.

Jesus gets yet another "Birthday *and* Christmas" gift.

Bob is the only person who has ever given me a Christmas present
because Santa never came down my chimney and gave me a present
and now whenever I see Santa I have to be restrained (why I'm not
allowed in malls anymore).

Rudolph's severe drinking problem was the true cause of his red nose.

"An enlarged heart killed him. It grew three sizes *today*."

Bob is always on me about my cholesterol (says I eat too much bacon).

When Christmas Elves Have Nervous Breakdowns

Other things that can cause nervous breakdowns:

1. When someone's mother tells them vampires are trying to get them
2. When a dumb Court-Appointed Psychiatrist tells you that your only friend isn't real
3. Studying for the MCAT
4. When you know that you are constantly being watched but you can never know who is watching you

Bob says I shouldn't write anything in here about missing persons in case there is ever a big misunderstanding so someone doesn't try to use something I write as evidence against me even though Bob and I have never done anything to anybody and this is a private journal and no one will ever be allowed to read it except for Bob and me. Right? RIGHT? IF YOU ARE READING THIS, MOTHER, YOU HAD BETTER STOP AND GET OUT OF MY ROOM.

Alice gives some good advice for us all.

Dear *Pop Culture Shock Therapy* Cartoonist,

My friend Bob and I really like your comics a lot and rip them out of the paper every day. I really like the comic about Alice getting mad at the rabbit who is always late (why is he always late???) but I think you should have her attacking him with an ax or a gun or something (you have lots of comics with axes, Bob noticed), and he could be dead and lying on the ground all dead (but his clock would still be working! FUNNY!). Bob and I could write comic ideas and send them to you because we have lots of good ideas. Or if you just send me your address Bob and I can come visit you sometime. Could you please e-mail me your address? Bob and I could just sleep on your couch. Please e-mail me your address.

Thank you,
Dan (and Bob)

STILL AWAITING RESPONSE.

"Yeah, Betty totally wanted me, but because I was so into Veronica, we never hooked up. What the hell was I thinking, Jughead?"

"Some crows give him a 'magical' feather and tell him his big ears will help him fly, so he jumps. It's just sad."

This is why you should never try to practice magic. Magic is evil and is from the devil and using magic and playing with Ouija boards and reading Harry Potter books can make dark forces possess you and make you do bad things that you don't want to and are really not your fault.

"Can you tell me how to get to Sesame Street?"

Sleeping Beauty's biographer decided to cut things off and end with "they lived happily ever after."

Past New Year's Resolutions:

1. Padlock room so Mother cannot get in (completed)
2. Track down and go to home of at least one famous person each month (got in trouble for this)
3. Take medications (Court Mandated—not completed)
4. Learn to play the sitar (completed)
5. Make eye contact with women (not completed)
6. Not speak to anyone but Bob (completed except for Court-Appointed Psychologist—didn't even speak to boss at work)
7. Dig a secret underground hideout through side of basement (completed but turned into backyard sinkhole)

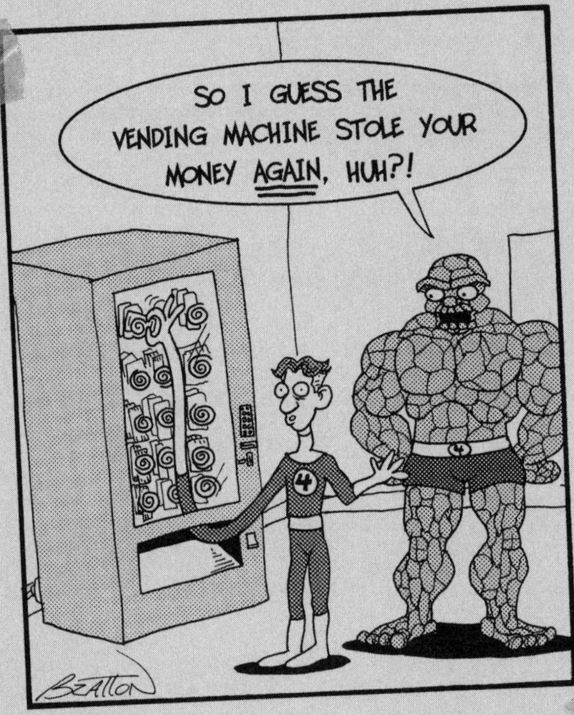
SO I GUESS THE VENDING MACHINE STOLE YOUR MONEY AGAIN, HUH?!
BEATTON

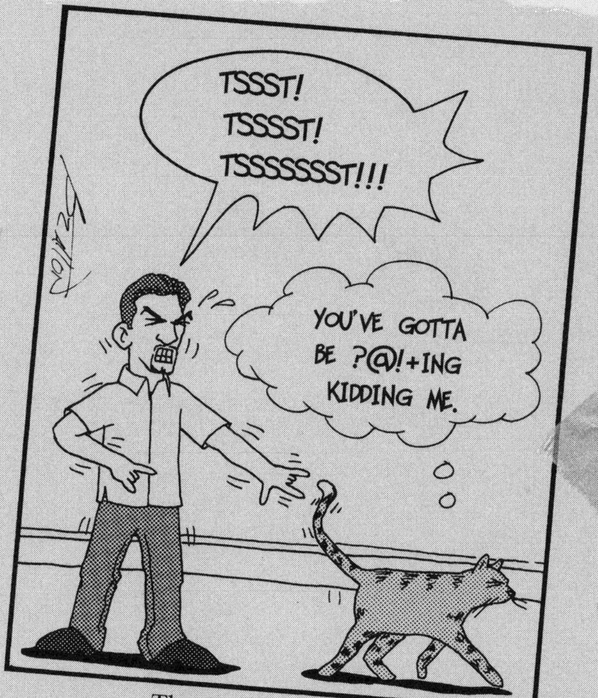
TSSST!
TSSSST!
TSSSSSSST!!!
YOU'VE GOTTA BE ?@!+ING KIDDING ME.
The Cat Whisperer

Indiana Jones discovers the Lost Ark *and* the answer to the "Where's Waldo?" question.

Dr. Seuss's Ongoing Struggle with Mental Illness

Bob says that loud music can help drown out voices but sometimes the people singing in songs start telling you what to do so that isn't always very helpful.

Mary Poppins's Job Interview

Exactly what I was talking about earlier. Bob likes to read
Harry Potter books but if I find them I burn them and he gets
very angry with me but it is for his protection. I like to burn
lots of things.

"Despite the instructions provided by Milton Bradley, your husband did not survive the removal of all his internal organs."

Gleek was officially kicked out of the Superfriends for "lack of heroic abilities," but the underlying reason was really his feces-throwing.

"We're going to a better place, Larry."

Irving, the Enabler

The Special St. Patrick's Day Episode of *24*

Court-Appointed Psychologist said I shouldn't watch violent programs on television. Says I should try to watch "positive" and "uplifting" shows that have good messages (*Extreme Makeover: Home Edition*, *Cosby Show*, etc.) but monitoring is too challenging so I can watch anything I want except pay per view shows that don't normally show up on your bill but the court can subpoena them so I can't watch those (not allowed to buy them on DVD either).

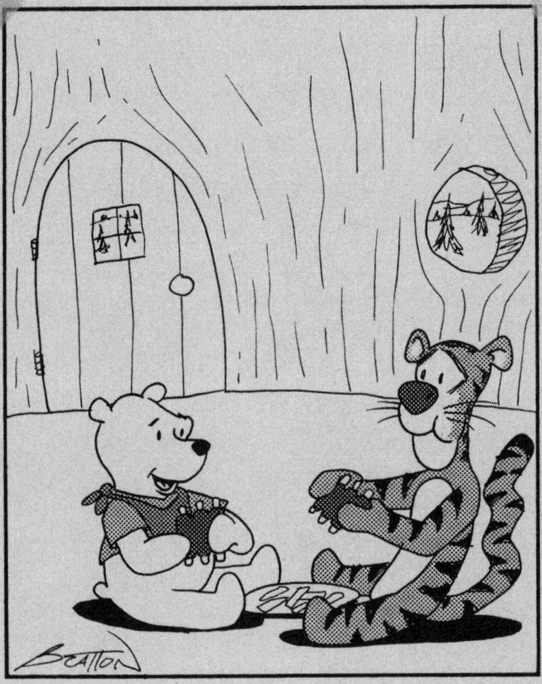
BEATTON

"Ha! 'Riblets from Piglet!' That's kind of funny."

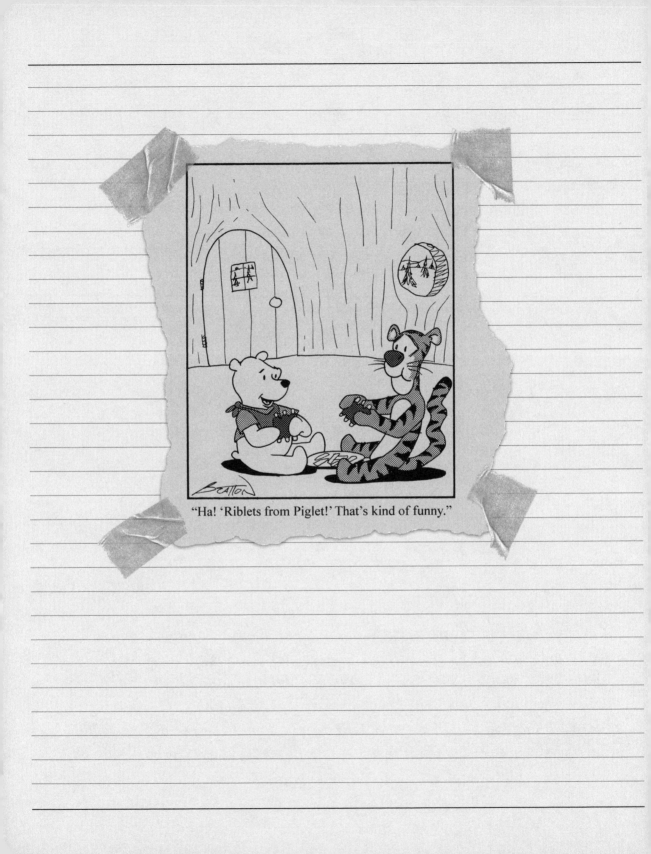

Cartoon Kids Say the Darnedest Things

Comic would make more sense if the Mother locked Dennis in the basement and his father disappeared.

Before he ate the apple, Adam never understood why he made everyone in his yoga class so uncomfortable.

Jiminy Cricket, before He Found Sobriety

Bob says Mother would have been nicer to me if she didn't drink every morning when she wakes up but Mother gets even meaner when she can't find her alcohol so I'm not really sure that Bob is right about this.

More evidence that Mother and *Pop Culture Shock Therapy* Cartoonist are working together. Bob and I got in big trouble for having a similar list in high school and Mother had to pay for psychological evaluation before I could go back. Bob somehow escaped without any problems.

Why Flintstone Characters Should Never
Have Their Fortunes Told

Pig-Pen was offended when Lucy misunderstood his interest in telephone dirty talk.

Things that make me want to shoot someone with a bow and arrow:

1. When people get ideas for their comics about you from your Mother
2. When someone borrows money from you for comic books and then doesn't pay you back even though he is your roommate (Bob)
3. When you have to wait for more than five minutes to see a doctor even though I don't want to be there but have to because a probation officer says you have to give a urine sample to make sure you are taking medications
4. When your Mother tries to poison you

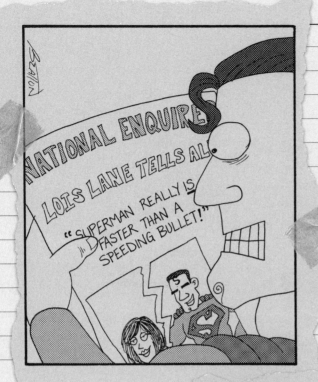

Captain Hook, When No One's Looking

And now Garfield hates Tuesdays!

Bob and I fight a lot about alien abduction. Sometimes people do bad things to cats because a voice tells them to when they take medications. If Court-Appointed Psychologists found out you did this, you would not be allowed to own a cat.

Muppet Gang Initiation

Awkward Super Friend Moment

Other things that Bob and I fight about:

1. Whether or not we should cross the state line
2. The toilet seat issue
3. If I should take medications
4. That Bob prefers to be called "Robert" (I refuse)
5. Alien abduction
6. Cats

"I think Mickey's drinking again."

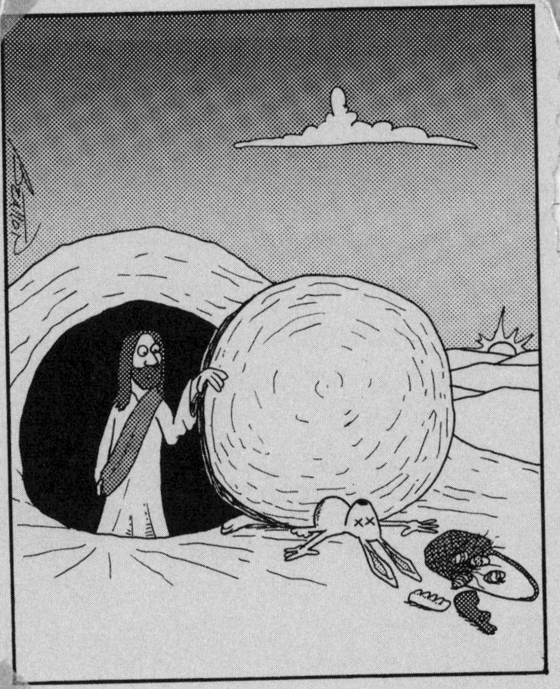

"Uh-oh."

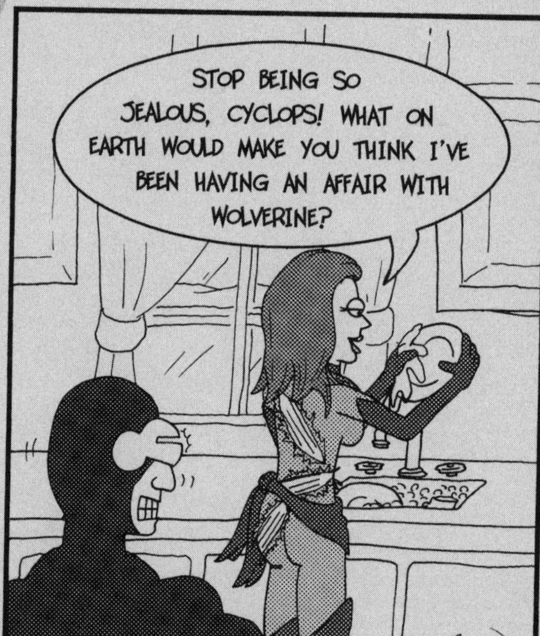
STOP BEING SO JEALOUS, CYCLOPS! WHAT ON EARTH WOULD MAKE YOU THINK I'VE BEEN HAVING AN AFFAIR WITH WOLVERINE?

Stewie Griffin in Play Therapy

Once had a doll that I would pretend was Mother and would stick needles in it but nothing would happen like it does on television. Bob says it would have worked if I had hair or toenail clippings to attach but I could never get close enough to get that.

Quasimodo's Family Tree

Monster Moms

Paper was always defeated by Scissors, and covering Rock gave him no real power. So he bought a gun.

Also not allowed to have scissors. (Would be easier to get comics out with scissors. Neater, too.)

Wii Lego French Revolution

Read a Tale of Two Cities in school but did not really like
it except the guillotine parts.

Ironically, the Hulk is a happy drunk.

Bob says there sure are a lot of cartoon characters who get drunk or killed in these comics.

Mrs. Dumpty knew that the annual Easter Egg Hunt
was a perfect time for Humpty's "little accident."

Eeyore's Short-lived Stint as a
Suicide Prevention Hotline Volunteer

Ernie's "dutch ovens" drove Bert to purchase twin beds.

Bob has bad gas. Usually people think I did it (did once—don't take medication while eating bacon) when Bob did it. This happens a lot when we are in public places (elevators, funerals, etc.).

Why No One Takes Hot Air Balloon Rides
with Crazy Smurf Anymore

Can't believe Mother would tell Pop Culture Shock Therapy
Cartoonist about the hot air balloon ride and police intervention.
THE COMICS ABOUT ME HAVE GOT TO STOP!!!

Subject: ████████████
Date: ████████████
To: ████████████

Dear *Pop Culture Shock Therapy* Cartoonist,

I know you said that you do not know my Mother, but I am compelled to write knowing based on certain situations described in your comics that you may in fact know her and get ideas from her. Case in point, the "Crazy Smurf" balloon comic. First, no one likes it when you call them crazy and it can make you feel very hurt and angry and want to cause harm to people because you are not crazy. The things that I said in the balloon were taken out of context by other people who were nervous about how high we were and they were never in any danger from Bob or me. Unfortunately, once the police are called they have to get your mother if you are under 18 and then she tells lies to cartoonists about you. I do not want you to write any more comics about me and I do not EVER want you to call me crazy again through the newspapers, as it is slanderous and I can sue you.

Bob and I are still huge fans and like reading the comics and trying to find your house, so please just do not write comics about me anymore.

Sincerely,
Dan & Bob

No response to date.

The Cause of Most Lightning-Strike Fatalities

Popeye's Nightly Struggle with Olive Oyl's
Eating Disorder

Edward Cullen: Vampire teen idol or
creepy old guy?

I am still afraid of vampires because of Mother.

Once again, Captain America had to bail out
Captain France.

Homer Simpson, before the Radiation Sickness

"I'm sorry Mrs. Potato Head, but your husband will be a vegetable for the rest of his life . . . Ha! That actually sounds kind of funny!"

Bob and I fight over whether a potato is a vegetable. Whatever it is, I don't eat it if Mother cooks it (because of the poison).

Dale does not understand double entendre.

Bob says that this line can get you into a lot of trouble, especially
with female parole officers. Also, I am afraid of chipmunks (out to
get me).

Ray Charles's Butterfly Collection

How Most Dwarf / Smurf Fights Start

The Tin Man Death Scene from
Indiana Jones and the Temple of Doom

Walt Disney: The LSD Years

Do not understand why anyone would take drugs, even when court orders it. Drugs can make you hear voices and make Bob go away and if hair clippers are around the cat does not like being shaved.

When Bunsen and Beaker's
Lab Experiments Go Too Far

More people should put pets in formaldehyde when they die. Then you can keep them near you! Bob says my jars are "creepy" but he never lost a pet and doesn't know what it's like to say goodbye and want to keep it even though it went to pet Heaven.

Tazmanian Devil Worshippers

You just don't tell some jokes around Superman.

Kiss's First and Less Successful Incarnation, "Hug"

Vincent Van Batman

If I lost my ear and the doctor could not put it back on
I would put it in a jar of formaldehyde and Bob would
not like looking at it.

Why Thor Avoids Superhero Public Restrooms

"So *that's* why boys want to grow up."

Bob says that just taking out this comic might be some kind of a parole violation. Told Bob I don't think this comic is even possible.

Why Iron Man Was a Bad Choice for
Dancing with the Stars

Ways I do not want to die besides melting:

1. Being eaten by sharks
2. Being poisoned by Mother (do not want to give her the satisfaction)
3. Freak septic tank accident (#1 on Bob's list)
4. Drowning in orange juice (it burns in your nose)
5. Razor blades raining from the sky

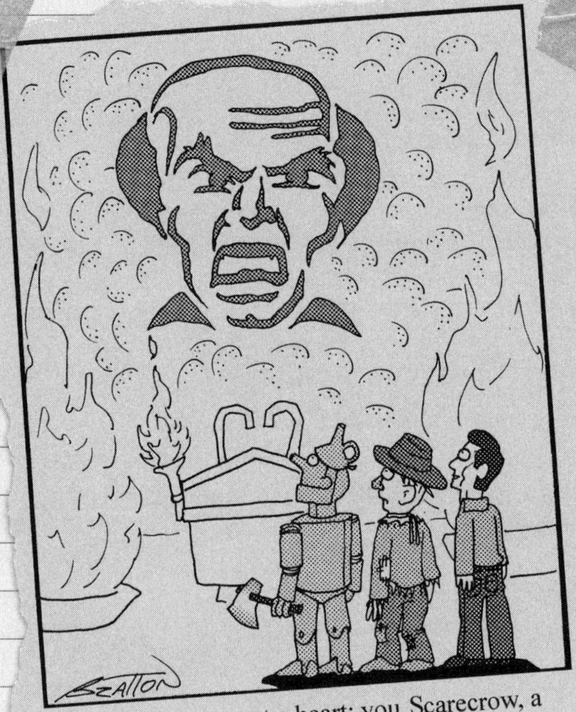
SEATTON

"You, Tin Man, want a heart; you, Scarecrow, a brain; and you, Ken Doll . . . you want a *what*?!"

Jim Henson's *Saw*

Not allowed to see that movie (court order).

After 20 years of dating, Irvin's criticisms became a bit blunt.

Other movies I am not allowed to see:

1. *Silence of the Lambs* (see below)
2. *Grease II* (Bob says it is awful)
3. *Hannah Montana* movie
4. *Psycho* (Mother won't let me watch it)

Dr. Seuss's *Silence of the Lambs*

Charles Schulz's Last *Peanuts* Comic

Tiger Woods never played a drinking game again.

Bob says no matter what happens, you never admit to anything even if you get caught doing it. And he makes me repeat that over and over again.

Hamburglar, the "Scared Straight" Speaker

Dagwood wasn't the first cartoon husband to lose his wife to the masculine lures of Mark Trail, and he wouldn't be the last.

The Old "Itching Powder and Kryptonite Dust in the Jock Strap" Prank

"Wait a minute . . . there are 101 all right, but
they sure don't *look* like Dalmatians."

A side of the *Family Circus* few ever see…

Dagwood wasn't the first cartoon husband to lose his wife to the masculine lures of Mark Trail, and he wouldn't be the last.

The Old "Itching Powder and Kryptonite Dust in the Jock Strap" Prank

"Wait a minute . . . there are 101 all right, but
they sure don't *look* like Dalmatians."

A side of the *Family Circus* few ever see…

What *Really* Not to Wear

Bob and I don't like these shows. They trap people who don't know there are cameras on them and then tell them their clothes are bad or their dates are too young.

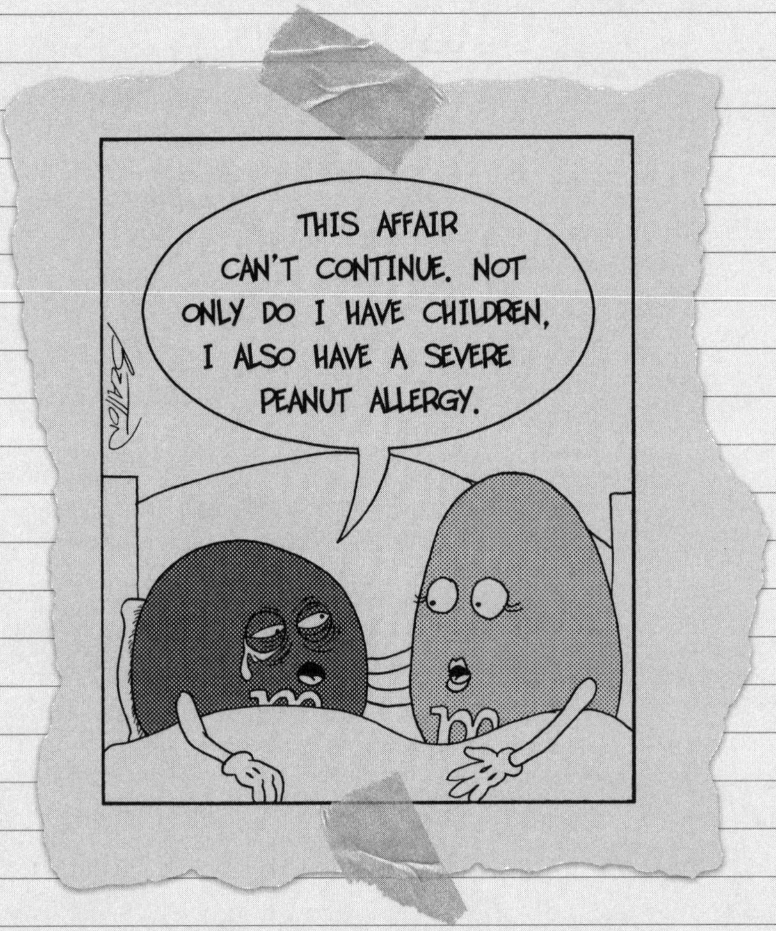
THIS AFFAIR CAN'T CONTINUE. NOT ONLY DO I HAVE CHILDREN, I ALSO HAVE A SEVERE PEANUT ALLERGY.

"It appears he choked to death on a chicken bone, but mark my words, this was no accident."

Lois and Clark: The Golden Years

Those are useful if you are sitting in the bushes for a very long time and don't want anyone to see you but you ate Chinese food for lunch.

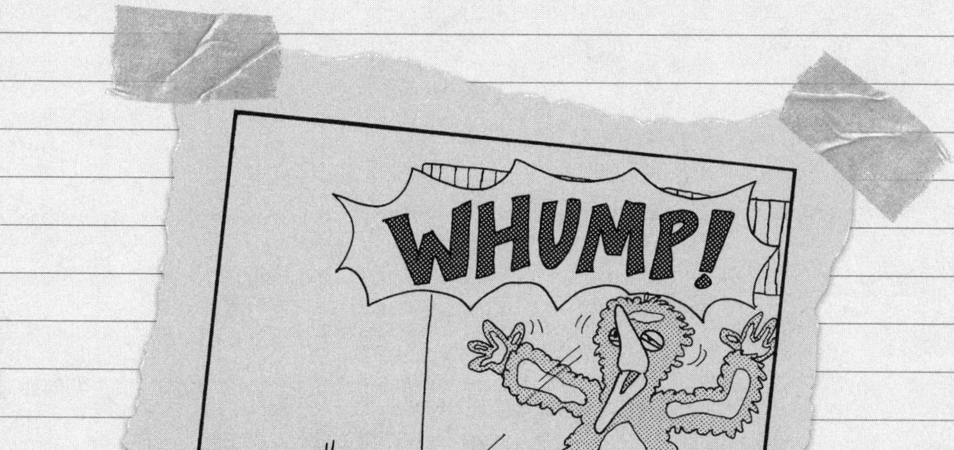
WHUMP!

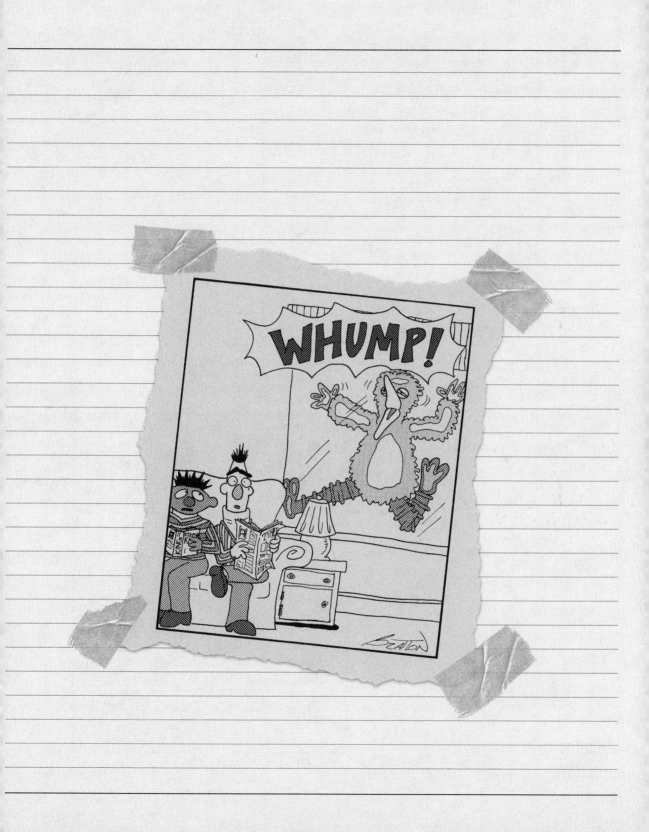

Disney Princess Women's Lib

M.C. Hammer's Invaluable Contribution to the
M.C. Escher Exhibit

Even Papa Smurf began to tire of Drunky Smurf's outbursts.

Drunky Smurf is funny but Drunky Mother is not funny, not even when she breaks out the clown costume.

Ewoks always got cast as Munchkins in Wookie productions of *The Wizard of Oz*.

Disney Pixar's *Down*

The Count writes his personal mission statement.

Don't even like Muppet vampires. The Count kept me up at night when I was 4 years old. I learned my numbers, but always thought he would come break into my house and suck out all my blood (no thanks to Mother).

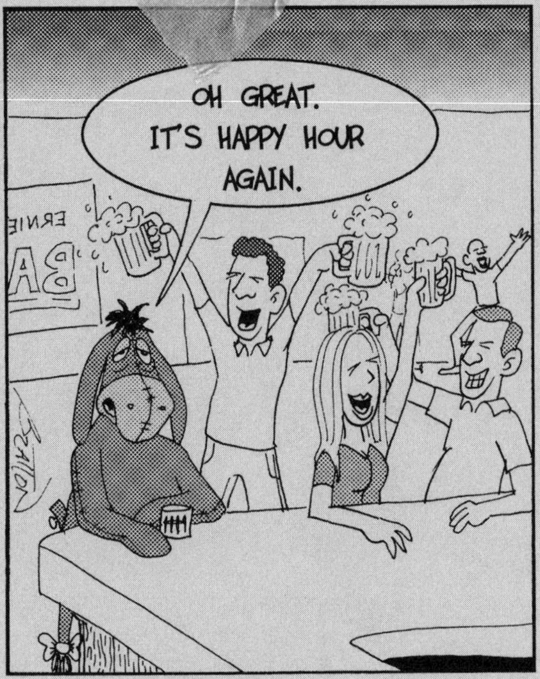
OH GREAT.
IT'S HAPPY HOUR
AGAIN.

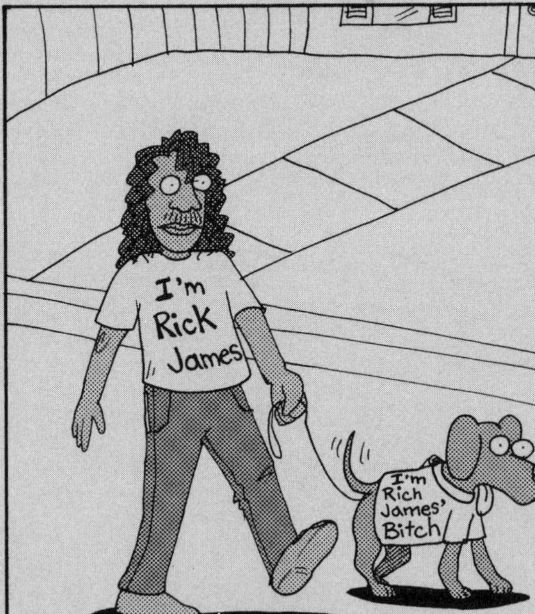
I'm
Rick
James
I'm
Rich
James'
Bitch

After finally being rescued, the class action lawsuit
between the passengers and crew of the *S.S. Minnow*
ended a few friendships.

Leonardo da Vinci hated Pictionary.

English translation: "Pull my finger."

Dear *Pop Culture Shock Therapy* Cartoonist,

I know you said you don't take ideas for your comics from other people but I think you do sometimes from my Mother, so Bob and I wanted to send you this comic idea (see below). It is funny like your comics and I think people would think it is funny if you drew it. You can use our drawing if you want to but please don't forget to write that Bob and I did the comic.

Thank you,
Dan (and Bob)

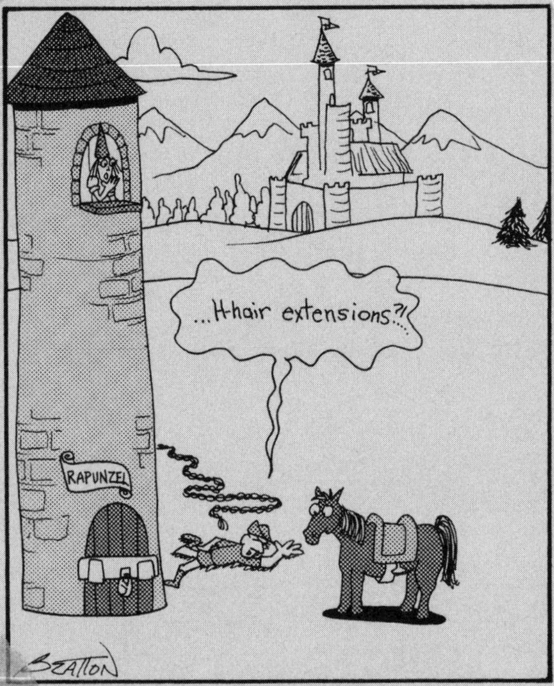
...H-hair extensions?!
RAPUNZEL

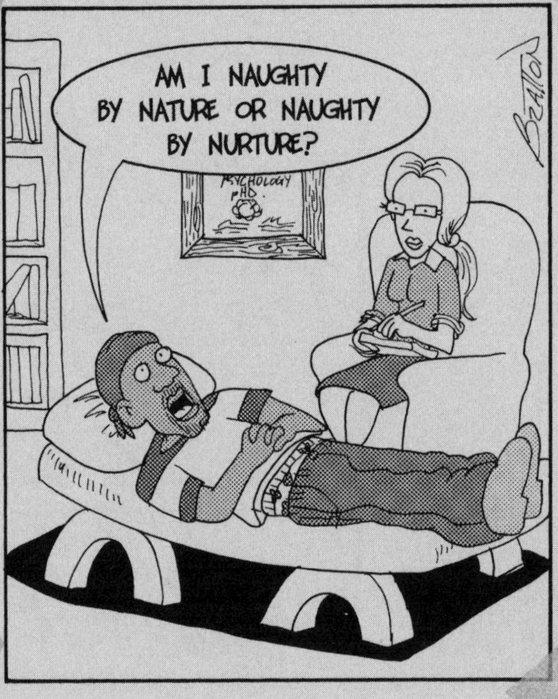
AM I NAUGHTY BY NATURE OR NAUGHTY BY NURTURE?

This would be a fun convention to go to, but I am not allowed to travel. (Another parole violation.)

Snoopy also successfully landed his plane into the Hudson River, but to much less fanfare.

Mrs. "The Frog" catches her husband and Miss Piggy in bed—totally naked.

Sometimes I wish I was a Muppet because you could talk to people with your hand and not have to worry about them making eye contact with you.

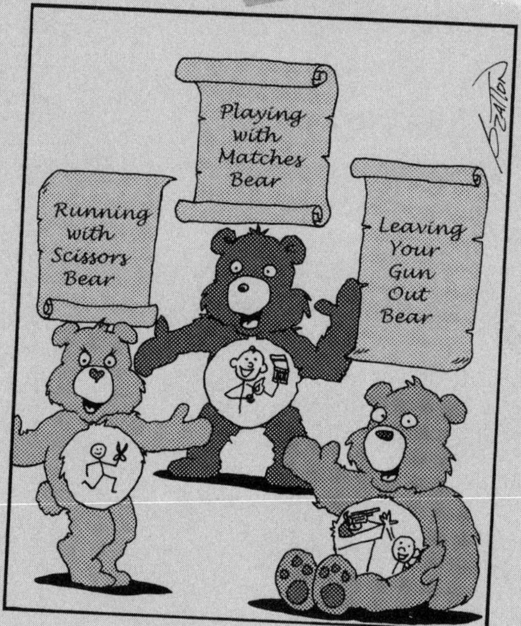
Running with Scissors Bear
Playing with Matches Bear
Leaving Your Gun Out Bear

The Careless Bears

Dear *Pop Culture Shock Therapy* Cartoonist,

You did not write me back after my last e-mail, which did not make Bob and me happy and I already asked you if my Mother told you the ideas that I had written and perhaps other stories about me that were not true. I told you that I had come up with other Care Bear ideas and one of them was Fire Starter Bear, which looks a lot like your Playing with Matches Bear. I think that you are getting ideas from me and that you should start writing my name in your comics because I thought of the ideas.

I think that the Care Bear company should also start using my ideas and pay me money for them because they would probably sell a lot of them. Do you get a lot of money for your comics? Maybe you could pay me to send you ideas that you can use. Speaking of which, I sent you a comic that I wrote in the mail and did not hear back from you. Can you please make a comic out of my idea and put my name on it because it was my idea? You could also mail me a check. How much can you pay me for each comic I write? I was thinking maybe one thousand dollars.

Bob and I really like your comics, but I think you should acknowledge when you get your ideas from me and give me money for my ideas. Also, I still plan to stop by and say "hi" someday, but I need a plane ticket to fly out to New Jersey (found out where you live!). Can you send me a ticket or money for a ticket? Two tickets would be better so Bob and I can both come.

Sincerely,
Dan

NOTICE OF MOTION FOR TEMPORARY RESTRAINING ORDER

ISSUED BY THE CIRCUIT COURT OF MORRISTOWN, NEW JERSEY

MR. DOUGLAS M. BRATTON and THE FAMILY OF
POP CULTURE SHOCK THERAPY Inc.
XX XXXXXXXX DR.
XXXXXXXX, NJ XXXXX

    Plaintiffs,

v.

DANIEL XXXXXXXXX
XXX-X XXXXXXX ST.
XXXXX, OH XXXXX

    Defendant,

                            CIVIC ACTION NO. 2010-3-11-D

To the Above-Named Defendant:

    You are hereby lawfully and dutifully notified by the Plaintiffs that said Plaintiff, Mr. Douglas M. Bratton and the family of Mr. Douglas M. Bratton will make motion to the Circuit Court of Morristown, New Jersey, for a temporary Order of Restraint against the Above-Named Defendant. This Motion will be made at Court before the Hon. Judge XXXXX XXXXXXXX on the XX day of XXXXXXXX, 2010, at XX:XX a.m., at which time you are at liberty to appear and demonstrate cause, if you are so able to do so, why the Motion of Temporary Restraint should not be granted by the Court.

        MR. DOUGLAS M. BRATTON and THE FAMILY OF
POP CULTURE SHOCK THERAPY Inc.
XX XXXXXXXX DR.
XXXXXXXX, NJ XXXXX

REPRESENTED BY: RICCOBONNO SCHIRMER O'BEIRNE & STORMS, ESQ.

SIGNED: XXXXXXXXXXXXX
    Joseph Evensen (NJ Bar # XXXX)
    XXX XXXXXXXX Blvd.
    Suite XXX
    XXXXXXXXX, New Jersey XXXXX-XXXX

When Luigi First Became Worried About
Mario's Drug Use

Bret Michaels was definitely "in."

Five Years after Harry Potter
Dropped Out of Hogwarts

Never had a blanket talk to me, but a candle did one time and I ended up burning my ear. DON'T EVER LISTEN TO CANDLES EVEN IF THEY ARE WARM AND GLOWY.

Mr. Potato Head's agent would second-guess
the *Iron Chef* booking for many years.

Oscar the Grouch's more successful kid brother,
Larry the Annoyingly Happy

"Lemme tell ya . . . livin' in a pineapple under the sea reeeeeeally bites."

I do not think people who don't have to live with a Mother who throws firecrackers at them and puts poison in their food should complain about where they live because they actually have it pretty good.

How Most Newspaper Comic
Barroom Brawls Begin

Insurance regulations required Dopey to wear a helmet and use a rubber mallet in the mines.

Sesame Street 'Roid Rage

The long, harsh winters finally drove Geppetto insane.

I like this comic because it has fire in it and I like fire until it burns me and then I get angry. But it is so pretty and glowy that I stop being angry and just want to light other things on fire to watch how pretty it looks when it burns.

Unlocking the Psychology Behind Dagwood's
Appetite for Freakishly Large Sandwiches

Conversation started to grow stale after a couple
of years.

How the King Landed His Mascot Gig

This is what Mother usually looks like except she is about 100 pounds heavier and wears sweatsuits (or sometimes a clown costume).

Why Alfred Finally Quit

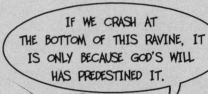

Before Bill Watterson transformed his main characters into an obnoxious six-year-old and a stuffed tiger, *Calvin and Hobbes* pretty much stunk.

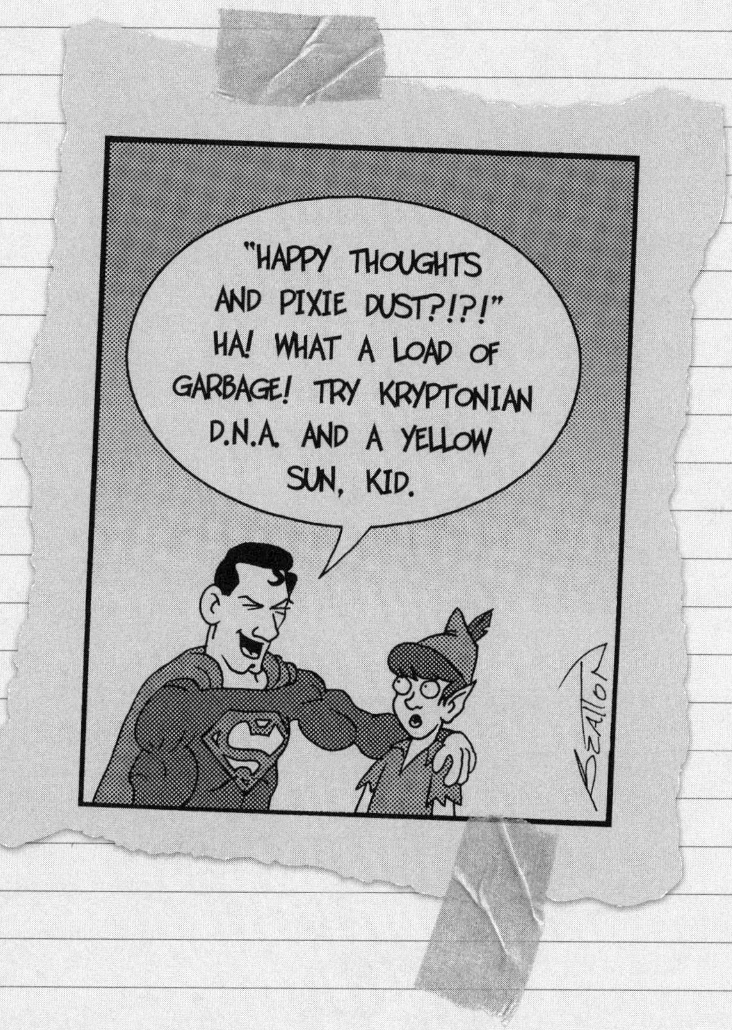
"HAPPY THOUGHTS AND PIXIE DUST?!?!" HA! WHAT A LOAD OF GARBAGE! TRY KRYPTONIAN D.N.A. AND A YELLOW SUN, KID.
BEALLOR

Christmas just wasn't the same after the elves unionized.

Sadly, Ralphie ended up shooting both his eyes out.

The Fourth Wiseman brought the gift of product licensing.

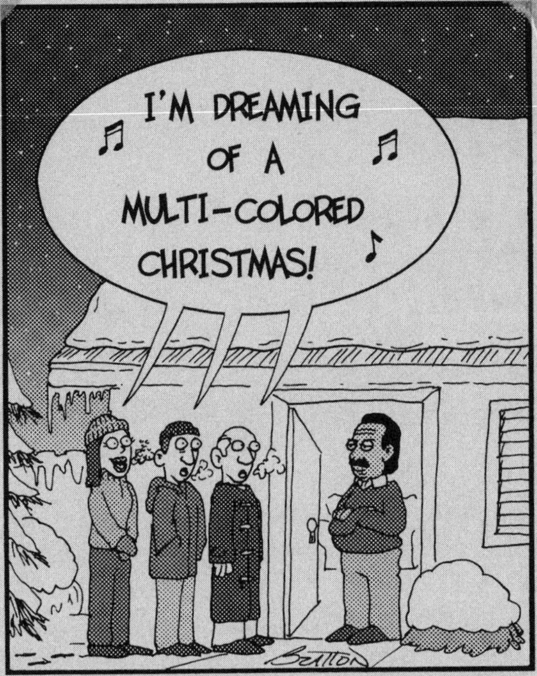
I'M DREAMING OF A MULTI-COLORED CHRISTMAS!

After the previous year's allegations of racism, carolers made a slight lyric modification when singing for Al Sharpton.

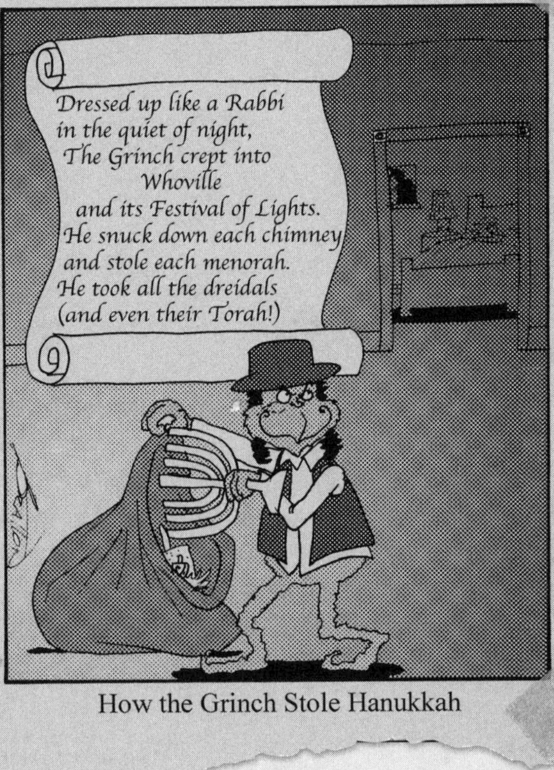
Dressed up like a Rabbi
in the quiet of night,
The Grinch crept into
Whoville
and its Festival of Lights.
He snuck down each chimney
and stole each menorah.
He took all the dreidals
(and even their Torah!)

How the Grinch Stole Hanukkah

Quasimodo's mom had an unfortunate pregnancy craving.

Bob says he thinks that Mother is nice when she is not drinking and says that her trying to poison me is all in my head and that he thinks I have a hard time telling what is real and what is imaginary and then he gets a sly grin but I'm not sure why.

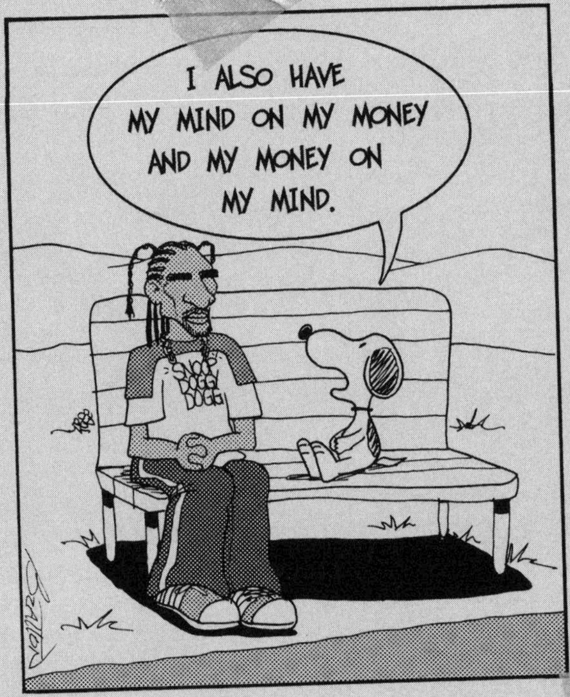
I ALSO HAVE MY MIND ON MY MONEY AND MY MONEY ON MY MIND.
SNOOP DOGGY DOGG

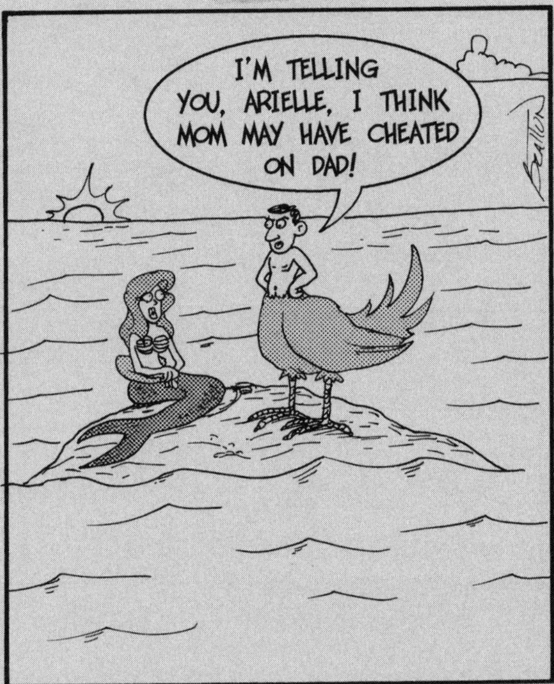
I'M TELLING YOU, ARIELLE, I THINK MOM MAY HAVE CHEATED ON DAD!

The Ewok / Care Bear War was short.

Bob says this guy sure does a lot of Care Bear comics.

Buffy ruins the *Twilight* franchise.

Pre-Teenage Mutant Karate Student Turtles

Bob says we should learn Spanish in case we ever need to leave the country quickly since I am not allowed to have a passport or take plane flights (because of hot air balloon incident).

Frankenstein's Post-Mortem Depression

Very angry at Bob. He read this cartoon and said that if Frankenstein has a non-bald cat he should not take anti-depressants and I got very angry because I am sensitive about that and Bob said he was just joking but HE KNOWS I DON'T LIKE ANYONE BRINGING UP THE CAT!!! I WILL NEVER TAKE MY MEDICATION EVER EVER EVER EVER AGAIN NO MATTER WHAT COURT-APPOINTED PSYCHIATRIST SAYS!!!!!!

Supervillain Brainstorming Session

The Things Luke Skywalker Contemplates

Olive Oyl just wasn't getting the good tips for some reason.

Emotional Superhero Poetry Readings

"You're suffering from acute Vitamin D deficiency, Mr. Dracula, so I'm going to prescribe lots of sunlight. Side effects may include burning to death."

Not sure if I hate vampires or medication side effects more. Probably side effects because vampires are not real and because people make fun of you when they see your cat.

Bert's Mom

The amphetamines were taking their toll on Sleepy.

Spongebob, after Many Years
on a Crabby Patty Diet

Not allowed to drive a scooter (or any other motor vehicle)
because of side effects to meds that I am supposed to take
but do not take. Wish I could drive a scooter instead of
taking the bus with all the smelly bus people.

Cirque du Familia

Clark Kent's Bris

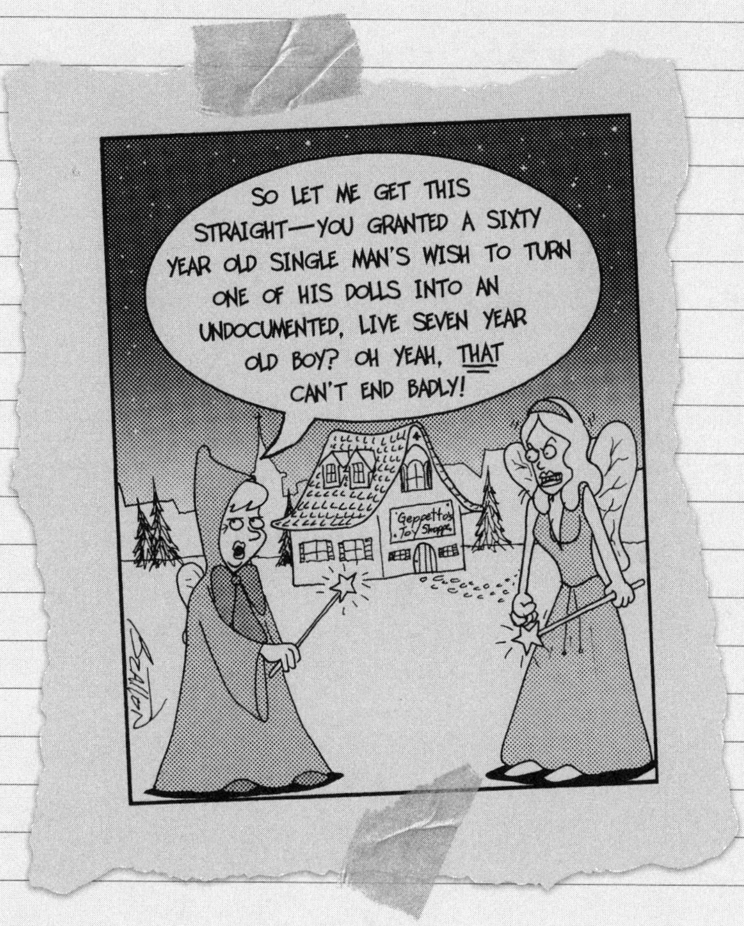
SO LET ME GET THIS STRAIGHT—YOU GRANTED A SIXTY YEAR OLD SINGLE MAN'S WISH TO TURN ONE OF HIS DOLLS INTO AN UNDOCUMENTED, LIVE SEVEN YEAR OLD BOY? OH YEAH, THAT CAN'T END BADLY!
Geppetto's Toy Shoppe
B. Allen

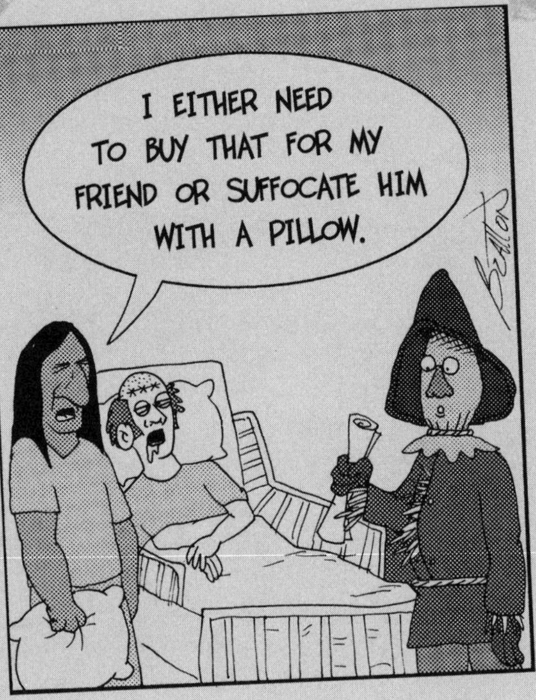
I EITHER NEED TO BUY THAT FOR MY FRIEND OR SUFFOCATE HIM WITH A PILLOW.

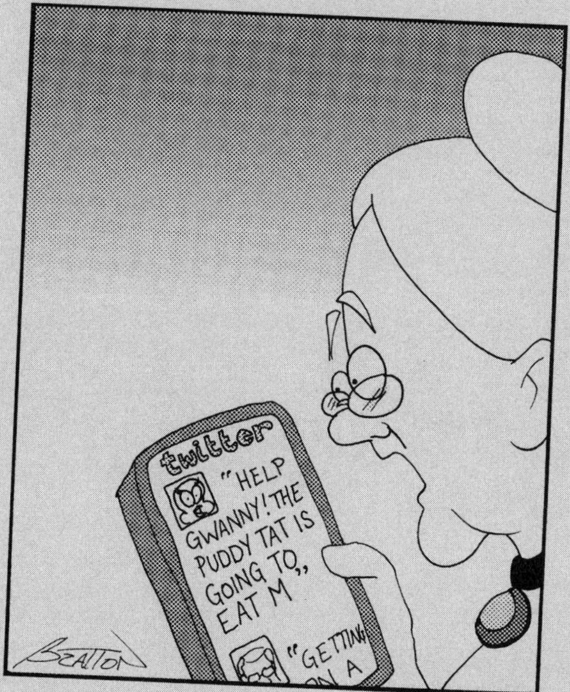
twitter
"HELP GWANNY! THE PUDDY TAT IS GOING TO EAT M"
"GETTING ON A

Tweety's Last Tweet

When M&Ms Contemplate Their Own Mortality

Bob says he can never die as long as I don't take my
medication but I'm not really sure what he means by that.

The voices in Jack's head just kept chanting the word "push."

Why do the voices always tell you to do things that get you in trouble, like "Push" or "Shave the cat?" Why don't they tell you to do productive things like "Go to work on time" or "Don't eat that egg salad sandwich"?

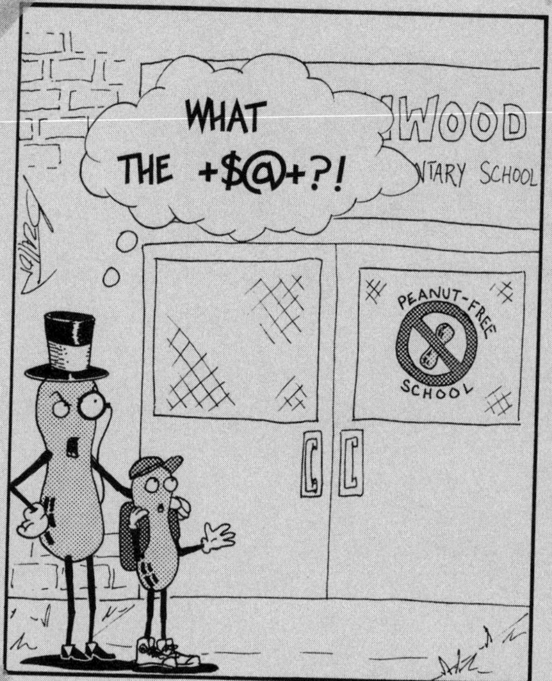
WHAT THE +$@+?!
WOOD
NTARY SCHOOL
PEANUT-FREE SCHOOL

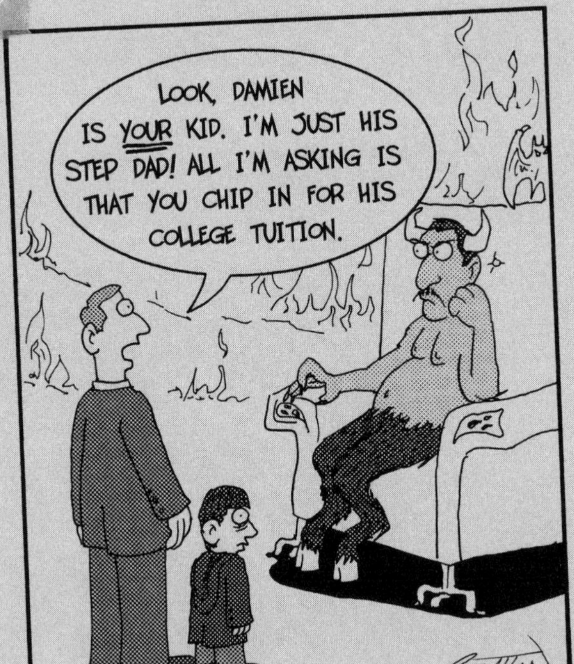
LOOK, DAMIEN IS YOUR KID. I'M JUST HIS STEP DAD! ALL I'M ASKING IS THAT YOU CHIP IN FOR HIS COLLEGE TUITION.

Marcie and Peppermint Patty speak out against homophobia in pop culture.

Rabbit loved to make sophomoric Pooh jokes.

Little Noah decided right then that if God ever destroyed the world by flood, and he had the only boat, no unicorns would be allowed on board.

SANDS
2008
WORLD SERIES OF POKER
RULES
1. NO X-RAY VISION
2. NO SMOKING
BEATTON
"Dammit!"

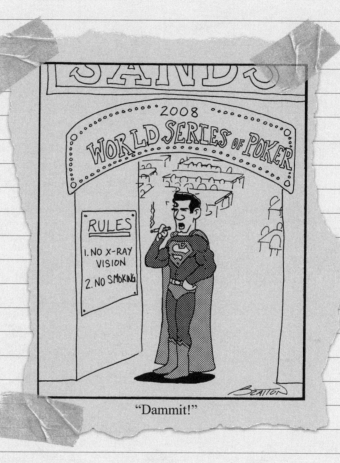

Eventually, Jesus decided it would be best to just move out of the college town.

It must be great to be Bambi (never have to worry about being poisoned).

Mr. Shaft: One Bad Mother Flunker

Why Batman's Job Is Never Done

Mother used to read me Winnie-the-Pooh bedtime stories but they would always end with someone getting eaten by the bear or all the animals blocking the doors and windows in someone's house so a vampire wouldn't get in.

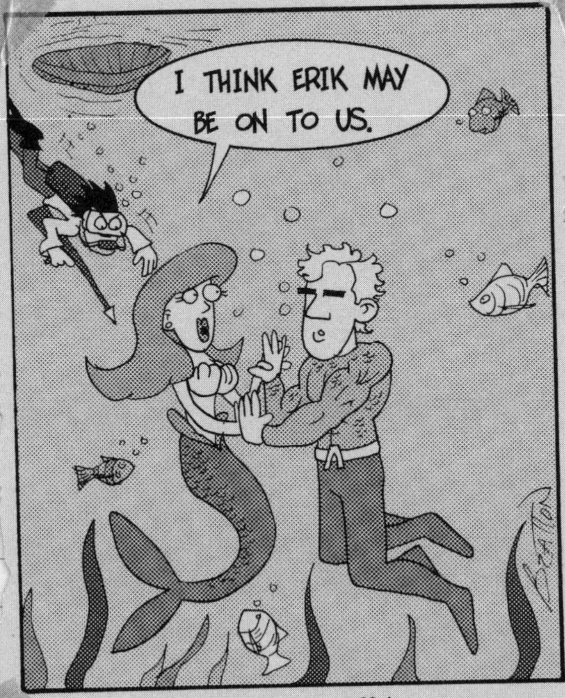
I THINK ERIK MAY BE ON TO US.

Under the Sea Affairs

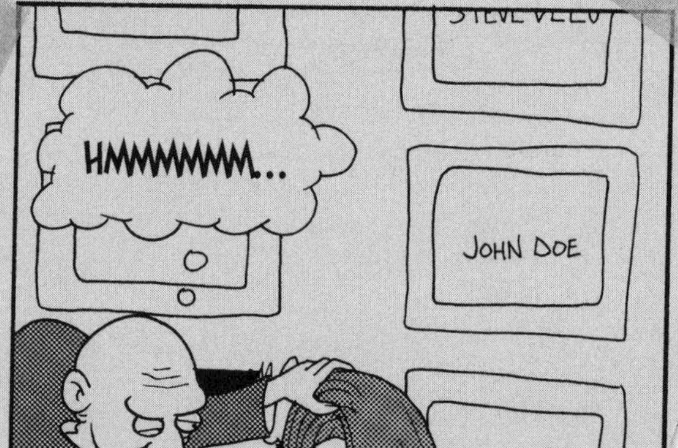
HMMMMMM...
JOHN DOE
JANE DOE
MAN FROM NANTUCKET

Igor's trip to the morgue for spare body parts would prove beneficial for Frankenstein.

Spider-man's Pick-Up Line

Bob says I would get in big trouble if I tried to get a date this way (using a net and/or mask).

Lex Luthor never bought Kryptonite on eBay again.

Once again, Lucky has a little too much green beer on St. Patrick's Day.

How *Dilbert* Ends

Understand why some people get angry at their jobs. I get angry at mine when people don't put the shopping carts back where they are supposed to go and then I have to walk all over the parking lot to get them.
I HAVE BETTER THINGS TO DO THAN GET YOUR CART BECAUSE YOU DO NOT BRING THE CART BACK TO WHERE YOU ARE SUPPOSED TO AND YOU SHOULD NOT MAKE ME ANGRY BECAUSE I MIGHT DO SOMETHING VERY VERY VERY VERY BAD TO YOU BECAUSE YOU MADE ME ANGRY AND MADE ME GET THE CART!!!!!!!!!!

Unfortunately for Mayor McCheese, the Jolly Green Giant had recently given up being a vegetarian.

Obi-Wan rubs it in.

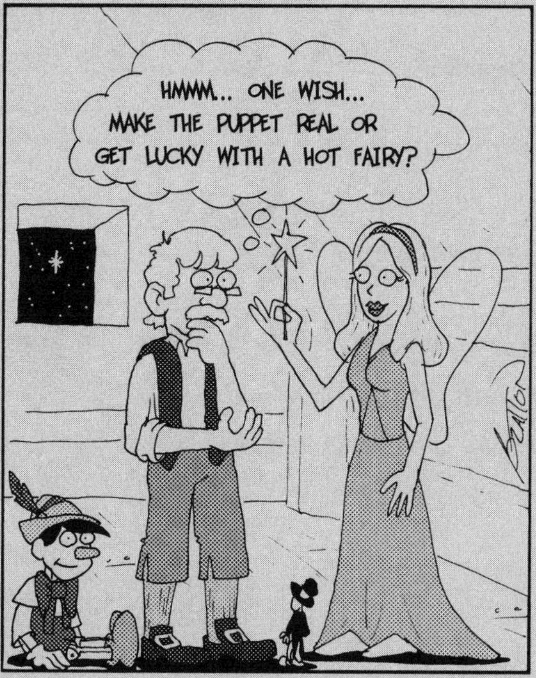
HMMM... ONE WISH... MAKE THE PUPPET REAL OR GET LUCKY WITH A HOT FAIRY?

Why You Shouldn't Mess Around
with the Space/Time Continuum

In his adult years, Linus became a fan of the Snuggie.

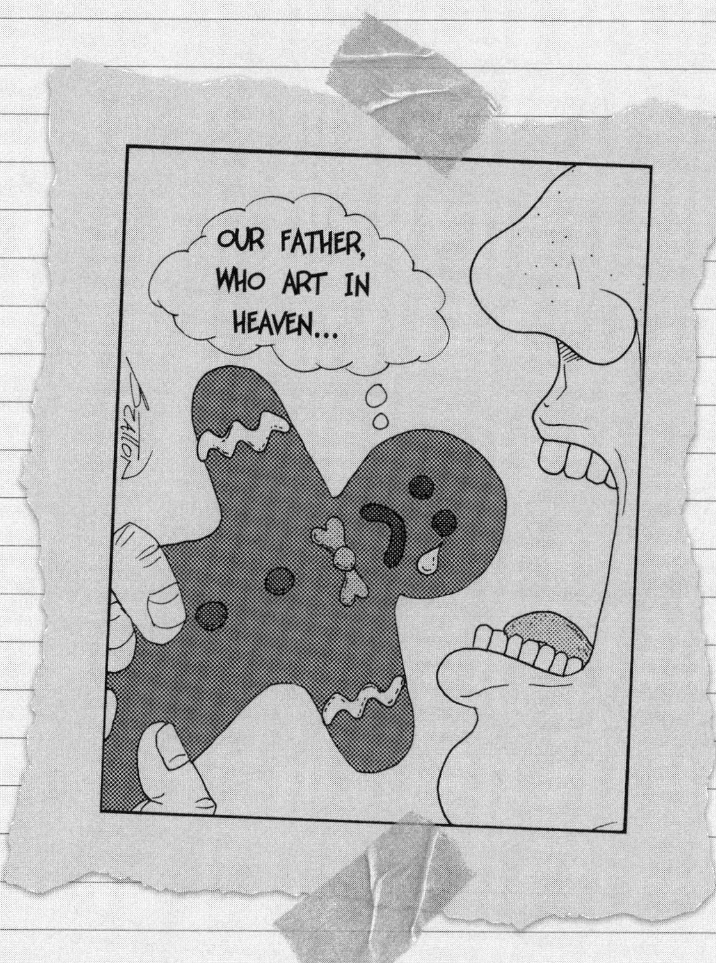
OUR FATHER, WHO ART IN HEAVEN...

Bob and I got into a fight because I said a **REAL** friend will shave your back and Bob says no way will he ever shave anyone's back and I asked if he would shave my back if I had a date and he said only if he could use the "cat clippers." Not speaking now.

Mighty Mouse was the Super Friends' first tragic casualty.

Marilyn Manson's Commute

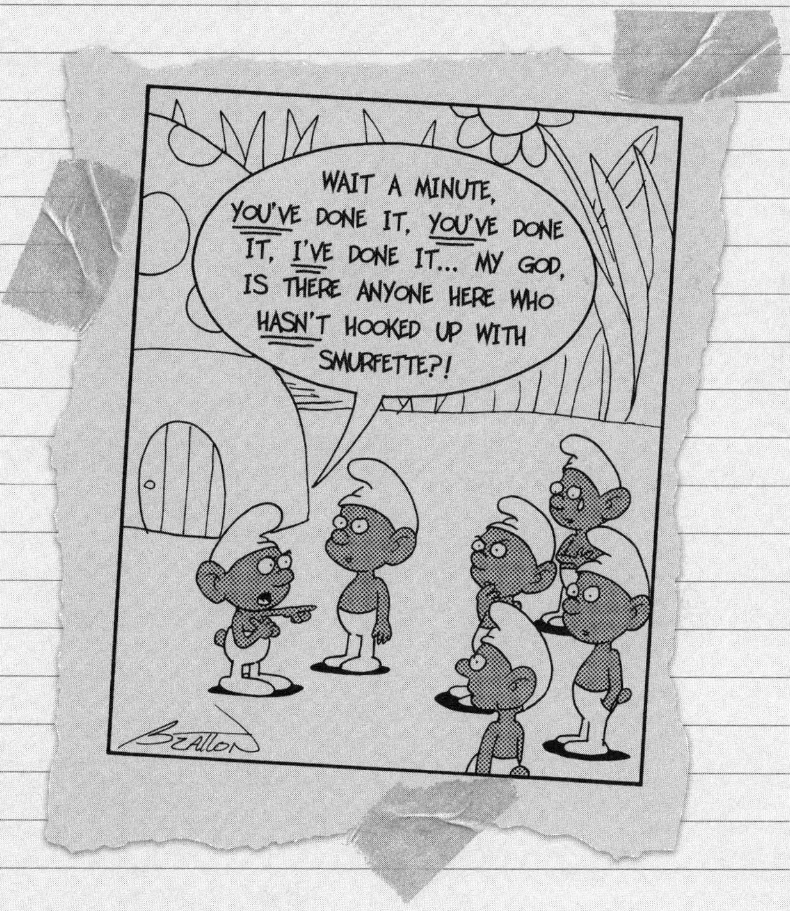
WAIT A MINUTE, YOU'VE DONE IT, YOU'VE DONE IT, I'VE DONE IT... MY GOD, IS THERE ANYONE HERE WHO HASN'T HOOKED UP WITH SMURFETTE?!
BEATTON

Garfield knew where to score good catnip.

After 30 days with no food, Twinkie the Kid didn't like
the looks he was getting from the rest of the Donner Party.

Calvin and Hobbes, circa 2008

Got community service for this when I was in school.
Bob and I are speaking again. Agreed not to discuss back-
and/or cat-shaving anymore.

The Questions That Keep Ronald McDonald
Up at Night

Grumpy walked into the wrong bar on the wrong night.

Snoopy and Randy Jackson

Huey, Dewey, Louie, and Stewie

When Cartoon Characters Take Their
Proper Medication

UNREALISTIC DEPICTION OF TAKING MEDICATIONS!!! THERE
ARE SIDE EFFECTS AND VOICES AND FRIENDS DISAPPEAR!!! I
DO NOT LIKE IT WHEN CARTOONISTS MAKE UNREALISTIC
COMICS AND I DO NOT LIKE TAKING MEDICATION!!!!!!!!!

Rollin' with the Homers

Pinocchio's "bluff tell" ultimately does him in at the *World Series of Poker*.

Wrote another comic, but this one is for me and Bob and not
Pop Culture Shock Therapy Cartoonist who does not e-mail me back
and gets restraining orders.

Admirals who interrupted Darth Vader's bubble blowing were instantly killed.

How the Grinch Stole New Year's Eve

Dr. Evil and Mr. Bigglesworth agreed never to speak of
the "mini bar and electric hair clipper incident" again.

Suspicions confirmed! Pop Culture Shock Therapy Cartoonist knows
Mother. SHE TOLD HIM THE CAT STORY. WHY DOES EVERYONE
WANT TO WATCH ME AND DRAW COMICS ABOUT ME AND LAUGH
AT ME AND TRY AND POISON ME?!?!?! Court-Appointed Psychologist
says they are not but they are! Court-Appointed Psychologist says,
"Paranoid delusions are a common symptom of BLAH BLAH BLAH BLAH
BLAH" then he rambles on and on. I just tune that right out.

Dear *Pop Culture Shock Therapy* Cartoonist,

DO YOU KNOW ███████████? SHE IS MY MOTHER BUT YOU ALREADY KNOW THAT, DO NOT LIE I KNOW THAT YOU KNOW HER AND SHE SAYS BAD THINGS ABOUT ME THAT ARE NOT TRUE (SUCH AS THINGS ABOUT CHIPMUNKS AND CHRISTMAS LIGHTS). DO NOT BELIEVE THE LIES! SHE IS BAD AND IS A LIAR AND WANTS TO MAKE PEOPLE THINK BAD THINGS ABOUT ME AND POISON ME SO I AM DEAD. DO NOT LISTEN TO HER LIES ABOUT ME AND MAKE COMICS ABOUT ME AND DO NOT DRAW COMICS ABOUT ME AND THE LIES. YOU MUST STOP NOW! YOU MUST HAVE MY EXPRESSED WRITTEN CONSENT/PERMISSION TO MAKE COMICS ABOUT ME AND I HEREBY DO NOT GIVE YOU PERMISSION. CEASE AND DESIST OR YOU WILL FACE THE FULL FORCE OF CONSEQUENCES LEGAL AND OTHERWISE!!!!!!!!! I KNOW WHERE YOUR HOUSE IS (NEW JERSEY) AND WILL COME MAKE SURE THAT YOU DO NOT SPREAD THE LIES ABOUT ME IN YOUR COMICS. BOB SAYS I SHOULDN'T HURT YOU BUT YOU MUST KNOW THE HURT OF THE LIES THAT YOU SPREAD IN YOUR HAIR CLIPPER COMICS!!!!!!!! (comic attached for your reference)

SINCERELY,
Dan

P.S. I am still a big fan of your comics just not the ones about me and the ones that are untrue.

"REVENGE IS MY ONLY VENGEANCE" -Dan

No response.

Popeye's Failed Sexting Attempt

Inglourious Basterd Birthday Party

Bob says I can't hit piñatas because anything I hit it with would be considered a "weapon-like object."

Dr. Drew, Bruce Banner, and Iron Man on
Marvel Superhero Celebrity Rehab

James Cameron gets greedy.

Bob has seen AVATAR 8 times but I refuse to go because I'm afraid the blue people might start giving me secret messages and it's PG-13 (have to get permission from court).

Joe Elliot was starting to make a certain
Muppet feel a little uncomfortable.

Yoda's Senility

Father / Daughter Troubles in Pop Culture

WAIT A MINUTE! THIS IS ONE OF THOSE LOUSY INTERNET DEGREES!!!
BEATTON

Death Row Records
Death Row Records
24
BEATTON
Suge Knight and His Peeps

My Easter Basket and Its Peeps

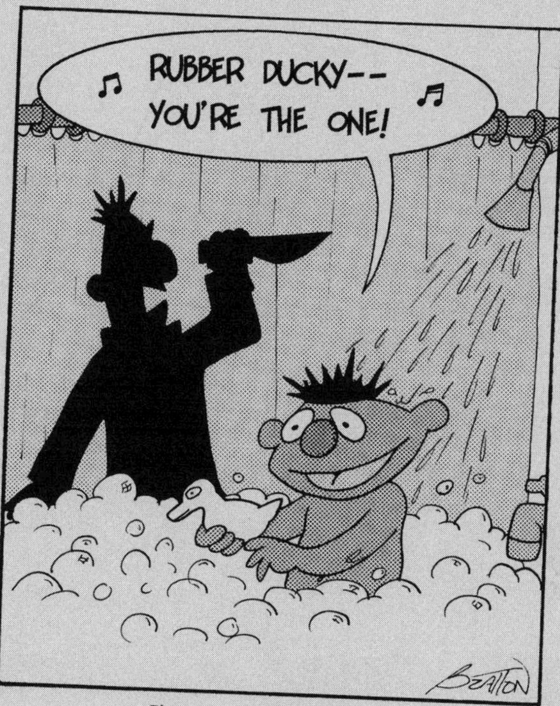
♫ RUBBER DUCKY-- YOU'RE THE ONE! ♫
BEATTON

Jim Henson's *Psycho*

MASON COUNTY BOOKING
AND PROCESSING RECORD

BOOKING NO.: 744 583	DATE OF BOOKING: OCTOBER 21, 2009	

CITIZENSHIP: U.S.	DL #/STATE: NOT APPLICABLE	MEDICATIONS: PRESCRIBED - REFUSE

ARRESTEE NAME (LAST, FIRST, MIDDLE I.): ▮▮▮▮▮ DANIEL	ARRESTEE PHONE:

ADDRESS: ▮▮▮▮▮▮▮▮

CITY, STATE: ▮▮▮▮▮, OH ▮▮▮▮

SEX: M	HAIR: BRN	EYES: BRN	HEIGHT: 5 ft. 11 in	BIRTHDATE: 1-31-80	AGE: 29

FILE #: 0603-71	AKA/ALIAS/NICK NAME(S): Bob, Robert

CITY OF BIRTH: Mason, OH	DATE OF ARREST: October 20, 2009

LOCATION OF ARREST: Residence (Mother's basement)	TIME OF ARREST: 11:45pm

CHARGE(S) FILED:
Stalking, violation of restraining order, violation of parole

SO. SEC. NO.: ▮▮▮▮▮▮	ARRAIGNMENT DATE/TIME: April 30, 2010 / 10:00a.m.	COURT: Mason District Court

OCCUPATION: Grocery Store Employee - Shopping Cart Gatherer	EMPLOYER: ▮▮▮▮▮

OBSERVABLE PHYSICAL CHARACTERISTICS: "Bob is my friend" written on arm in marker	CLOTHING WORN: Blue Jeans, Black sneakers, Black t-shirt w/ white skull

IN CASE OF EMERGENCY NOTIFY:
Arrestee would only say: "Not my Mother."

ARRESTING OFFICER: Huling #3418	BOOKING EMPLOYEE:	TRANSPORTING OFFICER: Easteadt #7418

CASH RETAINED:	PROPERTY CONFISCATED: Journal, box of newspaper clippings (comics), various weapon-like objects

OBERSERVER NOTES:

FOUR FINGERS—RIGHT HAND	RIGHT THUMB	PROCESSING INFORMATION:

Duplicate Copy
for
Doug Bratton

MASON COUNTY, OH
A P O   744 583
10 21 09

Acknowledgments

There have been so many supportive people over the years that I'm quite sure I'll end up completely and rightfully offending someone deserving of thanks by leaving them out of these acknowledgments. What do they say? Something about no good deeds . . .

First, a huge thanks to the folks at Andrews McMeel Publishing for their tireless work in making this book a reality. Caty Neis—thank you for guiding me through every step of the process, from my initial submission through the final revisions, and for helping the book evolve into what it could be while allowing me to keep my vision intact; you have been everything I could have hoped for in an editor. I owe a big thank-you to the design team for visually bringing *The Deranged Stalker's Journal* to life. Ben Vetter and the Marketing Department—thanks for taking the time to promote the book and for helping this newbie not get lost in the shuffle at Comic-Con. Thanks also to the Universal Uclick crew—John Glynn, Shena Wolf, and Paul Richardson—for, quite literally, inviting me to the party. Shena and Paul, I can out ice cream–eat you two lightweights at Ghirardelli's any day of the week (oh yeah, I went there).

Special thanks to a whole bunch of cartoonists who were extremely helpful in guiding me from the amateur ranks to the "show." First, thanks to the entire National Cartoonists Society (NCS) New York Metro Chapter—you have provided much-needed camaraderie, networking, and encouragement. Special thanks to Arnie and Caroline Roth for taking me under their wings in my early days and making sure I felt welcomed, and continuing thanks for making sure I don't get stuck with the bill at the happy hours now that I've ascended through the ranks. Also, to Dan Piraro, one of my cartooning idols who became a friend and mentor to me along the way—I can't thank you enough for connecting me with the Andrews McMeel team. Charlie and Rachel Kochman, thanks for welcoming me to the NCS when I hardly knew anyone, and also (Charlie) for connecting me with the Usual Gang of Idiots over at *MAD*. I can't forget Mike Lynch and David Coverly for making sure I joined the NCS club. Randy Glasbergen and Mark Parisi are consummate pros who were both incredibly generous with me, taking time to give some excellent feedback and advice when I was new to the cartoonin' biz—thanks for being cool enough to e-mail back an aspiring cartoonist, and for not just telling me my work was total crap, even though it might have been. A big thanks to Bill Alger for being my partner in crime with *Nickelodeon*—I couldn't have lucked out more in meeting you back in the Graphic Artists Guild's Cartoonist Alliance days. Thanks also to Kurt Marquart, one heckuva cartoonist, illustrator, and designer—your willingness to shoot me a quick e-mail about a comic you liked (or an idea on how to make one better) was and is wonderfully motivating and greatly appreciated. And a big thank-you to all of the wonderful people at the Museum of Comic and Cartoon Art in New York, for providing such a needed service to the cartooning community in and around the Big Apple.

Three *huge* thank-yous to the following: Dan Andriulli—for being so helpful with the Web sites, for being the best stalker ever, and for giving up your Saturdays to go to comic conventions and hand out *Pop Culture Shock Therapy* samples. I'm lucky to have a friend like you to sacrifice your time and help me do the things I can't do myself. Dani Pardo Bratton—my friend and sister-in-law who has answered more Mac questions than I can remember—for designing all of the *Pop Culture Shock Therapy* books when I had to do them myself. Also, for creating the "look" for this book—in a million years, I would never have been able to translate what I wanted from brain to paper without your design expertise. And special thanks to friend and book blogger extraordinaire Alison Skapinetz of alisonsbookmarks.com, for promoting this book like it was your own, and for guiding me through the world of book blogs. If everyone was as helpful as you, I could be totally lazy and still have great things fall into my lap.

So many good friends have been supportive over the years that it would be really long and boring for me to list you all here. However, many of your names show up in the book, so happy hunting!

As for family, a giant thank-you to my brother, Dave, for having a good (sick) sense of humor that has produced more than a few comics within this book, for catching my horrible spelling mistakes, and for just being an incredible, supportive big brother. Also, thanks to my awesome mom and dad for their love and support, and for trying their darnedest to raise me right—I apologize in advance for any complaints you might get from church friends who read this book (trust me, they're comin'). A big thank-you to the Melyans and Murrays—having great in-laws is a lucky treat. For my grandparents still here and for those who have passed—Grandpa and Grandma Huling and Papaw and Grandma Bratton—I cannot *ever* thank you enough for the love and support you gave to our parents, Dave, and me. You are my heroes. Thanks to Uncle Jamie, Uncle Don, Aunt Vickye, Great-Uncle Kel, and all of my awesome Payton, Huling, and Bratton cousins—I wish we all lived closer, but it's always been nice to know I have a loving family many, many places in this world.

And, of course, thank you to Pam and Caden, for all of the time you've sacrificed for me to chase this dream. I love you both so much.